We Are the Oldest People in the Room

Advice from an Octogenarian

Newspaper Columns
By Dr. Kent S. Miller

ISBN-13: 978-1727353471
ISBN-10: 1727353471

Dedication

This book is dedicated to three generations of Kent's progeny born from 1952 through 2017.

Three daughters and their mates — Ann, Greg, Jill, Steve, Casey, Ted

Eight grandchildren and their mates — Mary, Ashley, Christina, Carter, Elizabeth, Chris, Brooke, Jessica, Alex, Shannon, Michael, Sam

Five great grandchildren — Olivia, Andersen, Katherine, Kent, Cora

Table of Contents

Articles from 2015

Articles from 2016

Articles from 2017

Introduction

Betty and Kent with their first child, Ann, Austin, Texas, 1952

Kent and I came to Florida in 1955 with our three-year-old daughter. My husband, fresh out of graduate school with a PhD. in psychology, was starting a mental health clinic in Tallahassee under the auspices of the Leon County Health Department. There were no psychiatrists in town and almost no resources for those who needed counseling or therapy. Both of us were eager to find our place in a new community although we thought it unlikely that we would stay in Tallahassee more than a few years. Most of our family was in Virginia where we had met and married. But we did stay, had two more daughters, made lifelong friends, and lived here together for sixty-two years until his death on August 14, 2017.

He died three weeks short of our sixty-seventh wedding anniversary and three months short of his ninetieth birthday. I had known him for almost seventy years. He was a loving husband and father, warm and funny. He made me laugh almost every day I knew him. When he died, it broke my heart. That cliche describes almost perfectly the way you feel when the center of your life shatters. The most consolation I and our children could find in his death was that he was spared the long and disintegrating decline that is the inevitable result of Parkinson's disease.

Now for the genesis of this book:

During a long walk on the beach sometime around the year 2010, Kent and I talked about writing a book discussing what we had learned from being married sixty years, and raising and launching three daughters. We each began to write, but the book as we envisioned it never took form; instead these collected columns are the fruit of that conversation. They are a reflection of his long career as a clinical psychologist, a professor at Florida State University, and his wide-ranging interest in the world around him.

As an octogenarian, he approached the editors at the *Tallahassee Democrat* (affectionately known as the Daily D) about the possibility of writing short pieces on aging. They readily found a place for him and he acquired a fairly large readership. The columns reveal something of the man. He was a scientist at heart, trying to apply its principles to the social structures in which we live. He was also a man of action working to modify and improve those structures. At the same time, he was acutely aware of the complex ingredients of the human psyche and the emotional tangles that affect our thinking. Perhaps this heightened his sense of the absurd, his willingness to play and have fun, and his strong competitive streak.

Mark Hohmeister, Mary Ann Lindley, Randi Atwood, Martha Gruender, and Ron Hartung were all editors for whom he felt affection and gratitude. Kent was always grateful to the *Tallahassee Democrat* as the ideal platform to reach a local audience.

Shortly after his death, two people mentioned collecting his columns into book form. One was my friend, Diane Toole, the other our granddaughter, Elizabeth Riccardi. Dianne agreed that Elizabeth take the reins and move toward publication. Elizabeth then enlisted our son-in-law, Greg Riccardi; granddaughter, Shannon Hovick; and our daughter, Jill Theg. It became a family project. All spent hours on the computer and in conference with each other. This book would not have happened without them.

Betty Davis Miller
July 12, 2018

Rules of Life: Wisdom from the Poker Table

Once a month for over 40 years, seven of us have gathered around a poker table from 7:30 until 11p.m., drinking beer, eating, smoking, joking, and praising or cursing the card gods.

There have been significant transitions over the years. The cold cuts and the smoking went years ago. Blue Ribbon Beer has been replaced by specialty brews. In the early days, the host would get a case of beer to ensure not running dry, but now two six-packs will do.

When some of us began to have trouble reading the cards, we switched to the jumbo size. In the early days, it was a common practice to extend the 11 p.m. cut time; now it is not uncommon for somebody to suggest that we make this the last round at about 10:15.

Jokes about memory loss continue to be less common than jokes about sex, but the spread has narrowed.

Over time, the grim reaper has made room for new blood. Son-in-law Greg and his friend, Mike, both of whom started as fill-ins, are now the new yeast.

The stakes are relatively small but the testosterone in the room is still strong enough to guarantee competitive play.

So. What are the points of poker-playing that can be applied to the game of life?

- To get a seat at the table, you have to buy some chips. An investment is required.

- Keeping your seat requires accommodations. At 80, you can't manage everything the way you did even 20 years ago. Admit this and take the necessary steps to stay in play.

- The empty chair next to you is a reminder that, yes, indeed, it seems that we are all going to die. That awareness sweetens the day.

- Knowing when to fold your cards is crucial to being around for another game.

- We are social animals and need to be out and about — connecting with others, sharing our stories, arguing and supporting one another.

- The incorporation of younger players expands our horizons and ensures not being totally surrounded by all those old farts.

- The cost/benefit ratio of a given pot has to be considered. There are times in life when a small bet on a large pot is worth the gamble, and vice-versa.

- And, the most important lesson is that, even this late in the evening, there are decisions to be made, options and accommodations to be exercised. Pay attention.

Shuffle and deal the cards.

The Search for Grace Continues as We Age

If you are a senior who still browses through bookstores, you may be in for an unpleasant experience if you hit on a particular self-help section. Check out this sample of titles: *Are Your Parents Driving You Crazy?*; *Coping With Your Difficult Older Parent*; *I'm OK, You're My Parents*.

Then, turning to the next aisle, you will find *The Art of Aging*; *Aging With Grace*; *Rules for Aging*. The sheer number of books on both aisles brings home the fact that there are a lot of us old folks searching for a little grace at the end — and a lot of boomer children hoping we find it.

The authors of the graceful aging books have a hard sell because of pervasive diminishment and loss: sight, hearing, reaction time, memory, hair, muscle, balance, various body parts. Writer Sherwin Nuland points out that things that are supposed to be soft become hard: blood vessels, joints, lungs, heart valves. Things supposed to be hard become soft: bone, teeth, muscles, etc. Half of those reaching 65 have hypertension and three or more chronic medical conditions. Then there is dementia, with estimates that half of those over age 85 will experience it.

But wait. You know all of this. You're looking for ways to cope with it. Thousands of octogenarians are moving, going to the gym, riding bikes, making love, working, playing tennis, dispensing justice, volunteering in the community — and at least one can still run a 6:46 mile.

Robert Altman made movies at 80. Saul Bellow was a new papa at 85 (poor fellow). Former Supreme Court Justice Sandra Day O'Connor continues to teach and argue for an independent judiciary. Surgeon Michael DeBakey was still cutting on people at 90 (but not me). Studs Terkel wrote a memoir at 95. Wife Betty had her first book of poetry published late in life. These may be exceptional people, but they show us that it can be done.

At 85, the life tables project an astonishing six more years to come. Time for new pleasures and choices yet to be made. Also, it's time to relax. Don't feel guilty about taking it easy. If you are lucky, as we have been, your children will at least fake not having much interest in the books on Aisle 1.

Guide for Visiting the Children, Grandchildren

Our three boomer families are scattered across the country (California, Pennsylvania, Florida). We do a pretty good job of getting together but the spread limits how often we see one another, and encourages us to make visits as smooth and enjoyable as possible. This is the context in which I pass along some notions that have evolved over the years.

Of course any advice has to be tailored with consideration of the ages of the family. Easy for us since all of our grandchildren are mature adults.

Before an upcoming visit with the California gang we might get around to checking out what the three guys and their significant others are posting on Facebook. Not snooping, but as a way of learning what is important to them. We expect that much of it will be beyond our grasp.

As octogenarians there is very little to be done about our appearance. Our posture, gait, our everything, shouts that we are old. But we can do something about our behaviour and the way we present ourselves.

As you will see, the suggestions below call for minor actions (or inaction). But don't sell them short, as they can have a cumulative impact.

- Never stay more than 10 days, as you can conceal at least some of your major weaknesses for that long.

- Do not fall asleep and drool while sitting in the family room in the presence of anyone other than your spouse, who is used to it. But if you do, readily admit it.

- There is a high probability that during your visit you will be exposed to someone who belongs to a book club and you will be asked what books you have read recently. Your mind will be a complete blank. Be prepared by writing down three or four titles on a card you carry with you. No requirement of actually having read the books since the questioner is not interested in your answer, but wants to tell you what he is reading.

- Do not use any of the slang words or phrases used by your family, particularly the grandchildren.

- If you hear yourself saying, "Have I told you …," stop — because you have. Betty and I have worked out a helpful signal. When one of us starts on an old joke or anecdote, we stop when the other interrupts with, "When was that?"

- Avoid references to yourself as being old. Everybody knows it and would prefer not being reminded.

- If you have any residual physical competence, use it — meaning, if jogging or walking, go out full steam from the start, save the collapse until you are around the corner. Keep sharp on one or two tricks — for example, the ability to cut a deck of cards with one hand, or flip and catch a series of coins lined up on your forearm.

Take this with a grain of salt. You've made it to the 80s and your family loves you, and you won't be coming this way all that many more times.

Hit the Gym, Pump Iron but Avoid the Mirrors

It's 6 a.m. and I am at the university gym, third in line at the turnstile. My hope is to beat Adele, the 23-year-old student in line ahead of me, to the specific elliptical trainer that we both favor. If she stops at the front desk to get a towel, I am home free.

Sixty-five years ago, if someone had projected that I would be doing this, I would have hooted. The high school gym (the only one in town) was not a cool place to be, and bodybuilding was for narcissistic weightlifters.

My, how times have changed. Even the U.S. House of Representatives now recognizes the importance of the gym. In the midst of a recent scandal involving lobbyists, a resolution was introduced to punish former House members turned lobbyists by banning them and their spouses from the House gym. Representative Bernie Sanders felt this punishment was too harsh and suggested a compromise that would only require the lobbyist to immediately relinquish any machine that a sitting congressperson wanted to use.

But I digress. It may be saying the obvious when I tell you that I am not much into shaping the body, just trying to keep things moving.

If you are one of my peers and thinking about a gym membership, let me tell you a few things I learned early on.

- Avoid mirrors.

- Middle-aged men, total strangers, will say things such as, "You are my hero," which translates, "Look at that. The old coot can still step up on the elliptical."

- Attractive young women will make eye contact and smile, evoking a slight charge until you realize you remind them of their grandfather.

- Remember the earplugs, otherwise, your hearing loss will worsen. (The young are already deaf.)

- Don't expect much in the way of stimulating conversation. There is a pervasive air of seriousness while people count repetitions.

So, what drives me to the gym?

I don't want to end up like several friends, in a nursing home, unable to get out of bed in part because for years they resisted anything that called for movement.

More importantly, I consider myself to be a scientist of sorts and like to go with the data. Two recent books bring together the evidence that exercise changes the structure of the brain as well as the rest of the body: *The Athlete's Way: Sweat and the Biology of Bliss* by Christopher Bergland, and *Spark: The Revolutionary New Science of Exercise and the Brain* by John Ratey and Eric Hagerman. They say that exercise encourages nerve cells to bind to one another, elevates neurotransmitters, balances chemicals, impacts stress, anxiety, and cognition, favorably affects longevity, heart disease, osteoporosis, blood sugar spikes, colon and breast cancer, and depression. It is the medicine for what ails you.

In closing, I note that I have my detractors, people who know me and might ask: "If I am such an exerciser, why do I look and move as I do?" I tell them to imagine my condition if I didn't exercise.

One further benefit. When your spouse mentions some problem that needs your attention, you can say, "Can't do that right now. Doc says I have to exercise."

Don't Whine, Don't Bore Us—Take Responsibility for Your Health Care

Stop whining. It's been 70 or so years since you were a pup. And stop cursing. Accept the fact that you are going to commit increasing amounts of time to staying on your feet, not yet dying (but beginning to consider that option), tending to replacement parts, keeping the body tuned. Increasing amounts of time sitting in doctors' waiting rooms, trying not to get the disease from the guy who has been coughing on you for half an hour (and why didn't you move after the first cough?) and trying not to get angry because of the number of patients who came in after you who have already been moved into the back.

Let me give you at the outset one background rule: never talk about your experiences with the health care system. Yes, you will repeatedly break this rule, and it will cost you. You will be forced to listen to the boring stories of others who are set on topping you. It will be hard, but the more closely you observe this simple rule, the happier will be your remaining years.

The bad news is that you must assume more responsibility. If you are a typical 70 or so year oldster, you have five doctors and take 12-15 drugs. Your swamped primary care doctor is having enough trouble remembering your name (which is the main reason they have your records in that little box on the wall right outside the examination room), much less what four other doctors have done to you.

Taking responsibility means getting information. With any computer literacy at all, it is remarkably easy. Only a few years ago you had to gain access to some medical site before asking specific questions. Today you merely go to Google and type in a diagnosis or a procedure and the latest information is on the screen in seconds. Or you can go to any one of 60,000 health-related websites. (I like the Mayo Clinic.) In a typical day, an estimated eight million American adults will be logging on along with you in search of health information. If you are not online, spring for $20 and get one of the grandchildren or a neighbor kid to do it for you.

To keep from being overwhelmed, search for the latest meta-analysis on the topic. (A meta-analysis pulls together all the peer-reviewed studies that meet certain scientific requirements and summarizes the current state of knowledge on the given subject.) Yes, getting informed is going to take time. Don't begrudge it. And don't act as many people do. The latest survey revealed that the average time spent researching in anticipation of buying a new car was eight hours. The corresponding number for choosing a surgeon was less than one hour.

I have more valuable health advice for you, but my editor cuts me off here. Come back next week (or come by my house with a valuable gift).

Baby Boomers: Here's Some Advice for Your Future

Listen up. If you are an octogenarian or close, you can quit reading here. You have gotten this far without my help and these comments are for our six baby-boomer children (three daughters and spouses).

Dear Ann & Greg, Jill & Steve, Casey & Ted:

We frequently hear someone say, "We don't want to be a burden to our children." We don't hear anyone directly say they do, but from what is said, we infer that some would not mind being a burden as payback for whatever. Please understand that we don't want to be a burden. But it is unlikely that we will simultaneously die in our sleep after ardent love-making, and the odds are that at least one of us will be a problem.

When this happens, we would like for you to be guided by several basic principles. If we are reasonably competent, go with our wishes (e.g., with a terminal illness, we decide not to take nourishment). If we are totally around the bend, make any decision that fits without even a tinge of guilt. Yes, we know that the problem comes in the middle ground of loss. We respect your judgment and will likely abide by your call in instances that might impact others (e.g., when driving to the N.C. mountains is not a good idea). If we continue to talk candidly about the end game and our wishes, the burden should be lightened a little.

So. As you begin to suffer the slings and arrows that have been our companions for some time, we hope that your medical care will be as stress-free as possible. To this end, we remind you of a few things we have learned, small and not small.

Know to get the earliest appointment in the day so you won't hear, "The doctor is running a little behind." That if you want to find a good doctor, ask a nurse you know and trust. That if you can't get an appointment with the doctor until after Christmas, the best move is to ask for the physician assistant or nurse practitioner, who will give you more time and call in the boss with any doubt.

Get a young primary-care doc to see you out. At the end of any visit you should ask for a copy of the clinical notes. For any visit of significance, you should have someone with you. (We have done this for 60 years and continue to be amazed at the disparities in what we heard.)

We have had excellent medical care in Tallahassee but have traveled for expert treatment as needed. The President does, so in this democracy, why not us? You may recall that when I had a badly torn rotator cuff I went to the out-of-state center where FSU sent their most valued employees (football players). And I went to a joint replacement clinic for a partial knee, and a special center for radiation of the prostate. All with minimal side effects and excellent results. Keep this in mind.

It would be good if you join with us in advocating for a single payer ("Medicare" for all) health plan which takes the insurance companies out of the picture and returns the one in three health dollars they now receive as profit. It is the only system that is economically and ethically feasible.

Monday, November 18, 2013

Sex at 80: Intimate Relationships Still Important

Dear Reader: Be prepared to be disappointed because I am not going to tell anything about my sex life, and the Democrat, as a family newspaper, prevents use of a vocabulary that could be interesting.

Sex at 80: Yes, apparently, for lots of octogenarians. Or so they say.

Amanda Davis, 81, goes to an online news service to tell us what she likes. "At 81, I am still in love with sex and with giving and receiving love."

Davis probably is close to one end of a continuum and we can only hope that she meets up with some of those 80-year-old men that sex researcher Brenda Love says have sex daily. At the other end is a friend who says he has no interest in sex; the fires of spring having burned out in early fall.

The rest of us oldsters fall somewhere in between these two.

Reliable data on the sex lives of older Americans is limited, with the biggest advance coming from an article in the prestigious *New*

England Journal of Medicine. Interviews with over 3,000 representative older adults led to this conclusion: The majority of older adults are engaged in spousal or other intimate relationships and regard sexuality as an important part of life. The prevalence of sexual activity declines with age, yet a substantial number of men and women are active into the eighth and ninth decades.

Within the 75-85 age group, 38 percent of the men and 16 percent of the women reported they had sexual activity with a partner within the last 12 months (with half reporting sexual activity at least two or three times a month). The numbers are remarkable, considering the age-related obstacles to satisfying sex. It is also interesting to note that the rate of sexually transmitted diseases has consistently increased over the last decade for the 50 to 90 year age group. (Viagra came on the market in 1998.)

For those seeking assistance and a little more oomph in their sex life, the choices have come a distance from the eating of oysters, injecting the fluid from crushed testicles of guinea pigs or implanting goat gonads.

You probably don't need my advice here but I would suggest you pause before embracing the following "advancements": $10 drug injection at the base of the penis (ouch!), a penile implant, a vacuum pump, testosterone patches for women, $1,000 collagen injections at the G-spot (if there is such a thing and if it can be found), or cosmetic surgery on the genitals.

But to all of this, I say: if it works for you, go for it. Even if any benefit may be from the placebo effect. Give some consideration to the following comments:

- Quit worrying about how you compare with the norm. There is no norm.

- Don't leave this essay around where your grandchildren can see it.

- When you need some professional help with a sex concern, speak up because your doctor is not going to broach the subject.

- Being in a caring and intimate relationship increases the probability of a satisfactory sex life. What we are all looking for at this age is intimacy, with the physical expression through sex being a relatively minor piece of the action. Researchers at Oxford University found that kissing is a better indicator of a couple's overall happiness than frequent sex.

- Satisfactory sex is most highly correlated with good health. Take care of your body.

Make what you can of two recent events. Both the Administrator and the Director of Nursing at an Iowa nursing home were fired after patients aged 78 and 87 had sex. A nurse at the Hebrew Home at Riverdale, N.Y., asked the executive vice-president what she should do about two elderly residents having sex. His response: "Tiptoe out and close the door so that you don't disturb them."

Think About Late-in-life Living Arrangements

In 2011, the first wave of baby boomers began to retire, an event that deserves our attention because of some troubling numbers. The prediction is that within the next fifteen years, a fifth of the population will be over 65, and according to the National Institutes of Health, ten percent of the people age 65-69 will need assistance with the day-to-day activities of bathing, dressing, eating. The corresponding figure for those over 85 is 50 percent.

If you are filthy rich, no problem. You can find the help. But for most of us, a little hustle and planning should come into play.

Living with family is yesterday. Only 4 percent of American households contain three generations. (At this moment there is a slight uptick due to the economy, later age of marriage and other demographics.) As a next best thing, some elders have pulled up roots to move across the country to be close to a family member (sometimes finding that they are isolated in a strange city when the family goes to another location).

The most common move in our circle is to a transitional living facility, which takes whatever money you have in exchange for seeing you through to the end. The people we know feel that they have made a wise choice and report that their children seem happy to forgo any inheritance for the knowledge that their parents are covered.

Others have discovered creative ways of getting what they need.

Example 1:
Three elderly women pooled their money to buy a house that none of them could afford individually. The companionship and support that came with the move were much more valuable than the house.

Example 2:
In the 1960s, as part of a study of social networks, I interviewed retired snowbirds who had recently moved from the north to a trailer park in St. Cloud. Strangers, who over time provided comfort when spouses died, shopped and cooked for each other, in short, they did what was needed to keep people in their homes. (The county health officer complained to us that, "Those stubborn people over there refuse to give up their crazies," failing to realize that a group of strangers had melded into family.)

At the moment, we are hunkering down in the house we built 25 years ago, with all facilities on one floor, and wheelchair accessible halls and bath. Over time we have tried to build up a cadre of people (domestic help, reliable service workers, etc.) to help us stay in place, all the while knowing that dramatic change is lurking just around the corner.

As the aging process advances so do the risks of living at home. There are some promising developments that can help. We read that within a few years there will be machines that record vital signs and send them to the doctor or caregiver, a computerized medicine cabinet that guards against taking the wrong medicine, a wireless system that notifies a caregiver of the temperature in the house and sensors that record how many times a person gets up at night. All of this may be a little too much with respect to privacy and independence, and it is not clear who responds to all this information. Maybe that will come with a personal drone hovering over the house.

We encourage our children not to fret over our attempts to remain mobile and independent. There are things worse than falling, breaking a hip and dying.

Meanwhile, we should be working for policy changes that would make it easier for families to assume responsibility for their own, like tax credits for expanding space to accommodate a parent and loosening zoning restrictions.

Monday, December 16, 2013

We're a Nation of Stuff—Time to Turn It Loose

My friend, Pete, with his tongue not quite reaching his cheek, used to argue that in the end, the person with the most toys wins. He beat me out by a mile with his plane, boat, sports car, fly-fishing equipment and much more.

I kidded with him that it was his stuff that owned him, not the other way around—that his life was spent servicing the toys, learning how they operate, worrying about losing them, driving 170 miles to Jacksonville to see that his Mercedes received proper servicing, searching for the right insurance. But indeed, he knew how to enjoy them and did so up until a much-too-early death.

With Pete at one end of the continuum, I give you at the other end our friend, Janice, a retired social work professor. Several years ago she and her husband sold the big house in which they raised five children and bought a smaller one in a retirement community. Four years later, when her husband died, she moved into a single room apartment in the same community, her bed over in one corner. She just didn't want to be encumbered with things. "This is all I need," she says, spending a good part of her time counseling others in the difficult process of transitioning to reduced quarters and fewer things.

Most of us fall somewhere in between these two people, but at 80, should be rubbing shoulders with Janice, cultivating the art of turning loose.

Some people do this with great ease. I think of two male friends who have been in our living room many times. I would bet they could not name a single object or feature of the room. (Well, maybe one of them could have noticed the piano.) I could sit across from them stark naked and they would not notice, which now that I think about it, might be a healthy sign. They live in a world of ideas, words, and politics. With respect to material things, they are very much in camp with Janice.

But for many, turning loose is difficult, for we are a nation of things. The more we have, the surer we are that we are competent, successful, even patriotic. But there are lots of positives associated with having less.

- Things demand attention. Fewer things mean more time for other activities.

- You're less likely to trip over something when you get up at night to pee.

- It's easier to find your glasses when they have been misplaced.

- The smell of your closet will improve when the old clothes and shoes are gone.

- Some of the things you pass on will bring pleasure to others.

- By giving away some of your possessions now, you can be assured that they go where you want them to. Betty made an excellent move some time ago when she had our daughters rank order 10 things we have that they would like to have eventually. Where there were overlaps she instituted a National Football League draft, with alternating picks. We all know where these things will go and everybody professes to be happy about it.

- If you give to a nonprofit organization, there could be a significant tax benefit.

- Giving generally elicits good feelings for the giver.

- You will be doing a tremendous favor for your children or whoever it is that comes in to clean up after you depart.

Most of this is to encourage you to get with the program by closing the front door—never so tightly as to exclude essentials like books of poetry, flowers or 70 percent cocoa candy—and opening the back. For specific advice on how to do it, you'll have to return next Monday.

Monday, December 23, 2013

Get Rid of Unneeded Stuff

If you read this column last week and you are back, you must have decided to get rid of at least some stuff. Having opened the back door, I suggest starting with some easy tosses.

The lifetime collection of *National Geographic* and the 22 volume *Encyclopedia Britannica* can be dumped without the world coming to an end. Actually, if you still have these you are going to be a hard case, and maybe you should just go back to the ballgame now. (Confession: we still have the *Britannica*. That's Betty's fault, not mine. She says they fill the bottom shelf so well.)

Get rid of any clothes not worn within a specified time period—start with two years—work down to three months. Those clothes are never coming back into style.

Dump the frying pan you bought at a garage sale for $2 because you thought it was worth $27. You have a sufficiency of pans.

Tell the kids to come get the stuff you have been storing for them for 50 years.

There is no way you can read all the words streaming into your house. Quit feeling guilty about it and refuse the cut-rate offers to renew every subscription.

Books present the biggest hurdle. You remember when and where you acquired them and you never know when you might need them for research or a pleasant re-reading. You love them so much that you understand why Carl Sandburg had to rent a boxcar to ship his books when he moved from Michigan to North Carolina. Find consolation in the pleasure you will be giving to another reader, the good in supporting the Friends of the Library book sale.

Out with all those letters of appreciation, awards as most improved player, plaques of any kind, any document that begins with "Whereas." You know who you are by now and no longer need this kind of affirmation. We just returned from a visit with our California family, tickled by what they had done with college diplomas and things they couldn't part with. (They lined the garage walls at about the ten-foot level.)

Use this short list of examples as a spur to customize your own set.

Expect to have a few instances where you toss something you would like to have back. But the gains will significantly outweigh these losses.

Not everything has to go. And if it pleases you to see all your tools up on the wall, even though you will not be using them, that will be sufficient reason to leave them there.

On our first anniversary, Betty had somehow saved up enough to give me a Girard Perregaux wrist watch which I am wearing this moment (I gave her a $13 comb and brush set). To get that watch you would have to take my left arm.

Be sure to leave enough stuff around to engage the people who come around for the final weeding. It's something for them to do in the mourning process, thinking about your life for a day or two, possibly shedding a few tears and then getting on with living.

Gleanings from a Pocket Calendar

For most of my adult life, I have carried a 3" x 5" pocket calendar containing my appointments, phone numbers, passwords, etc. Each December I transfer the important stuff to a new one.

For reasons not clear to me, at the end of 1976, I tossed the calendar into a desk drawer instead of a wastebasket, and have continued to do so ever since.

When I recently spotted the 38 calendars on a shelf in my office, it occurred to me that they might serve a higher calling. For years I have worried off and on, just as I am sure you have, about Socrates' declaration that the unexamined life is not worth living. Meaning, I think, that for personal and spiritual growth we need to reflect a little on where we have been.

With the aid of a scotch and these calendars, I have reflected on my history.

I have had a really good time (lots of entries for tennis, poker, travel, movies).

Over the years the amount of white space in the calendars has been increasing. As it has in our lives. Each year there is less on the table and it is easier to shuck off unpleasant duties or requests. When needed, I reach for: "Sorry, I can't do that. My old troubles you know." No one dare push that further for fear that they will hear all about those old troubles.

My life is characterized by a surprising continuity. Over time the same names appear time and again. A lot of shared lives, good times and bad. Lived on Randolph Circle for 53 years. (Ok, three different houses.) Sleeping with the same woman for 22,995 nights (approximate). As I write, I am aware that all of this continuity could be subject to an alternative interpretation. Boring, lacking in adventure, missing out on the excitement of affairs, variety, change, a failure to draw on the possibilities of life. Maybe. But I did smoke a joint once in New Orleans with some graduate students, and not knowing what to expect, it didn't do a thing for me.

But the calendars also reveal the flip-side interruptions, the inevitable breaks in the chain. There are the names of people we liked and shared meals with but no longer see, simply because of the vagaries of life. Regrets that intimacy is possible with only a limited number of people.

I must have a form of mad cow disease. Spongiform encephalopathy. Many of the entries could have been made by a stranger. I must have a highly efficient delete button which is active through the day, moving to the trash basket that which is no longer of interest or value to me. The lesson here is that we need to keep in mind that the memories we store are highly selective, filtered by screens outside of consciousness.

Work in my two primary jobs has been highly satisfying. Lots of people think that professors work an average of about 17 hours per week, and the minimum requirement for a therapist is the ability to look wise, make eye contact, nod periodically, and ask a few questions.

Family has provided the major structure for my life. We have a friend whose daughter lives about 600 miles away and they see her two or three times a year. The friend recently observed that if she lives another five years they will see the daughter only about a dozen or so times. It is shocking to think that her circumstances applied to us, with family in California and Pennsylvania. The thought of seeing any of our children or many of our friends that limited number of times is sobering while adding meaning to the times together. But in many ways technology (easy phone contact, Skype, etc.) has increased intimacy.

What do I take away from this little exercise with the calendars?

My goal is to do the best I can to put the lie to Mark Twain's observation, "The first part of life consists of the capacity to enjoy life without the chance; the last half consists of the chance without the capacity."

 I embrace two seemingly contradictory sound bites from the Vonnegut family:

Kurt: *We are here on Earth to fart around.*

Mark: *We are here to help each other get through this thing, whatever it is.*

There it is. Try to have some fun each day. Go do some good.

Monday, January 6, 2014

Money Management After Age 80

If you are an octogenarian struggling to stay above water, or very rich, this column will be of little interest and I offer you an excused absence. In order for anything I say here to be pertinent, you need to have a least some money.

The probability that anyone who knows me well would seek my advice on money management is about as high as one of my sons-in-law coming to me for sartorial guidance. Our limited forays into the market were failures; we naively bought stock in December, taking a hit through an end of the year taxable gains distribution; the modest cabin we owned in the mountains of North Carolina we sold at the wrong time and had to repay seven years worth of depreciation. And the one time I consulted a tax expert was not exactly an alpha male experience. She looked at our papers, made a few suggestions and refused to take a fee.

Given this context, I acknowledge the chutzpah involved in offering the following suggestions.

At 80, you are in trouble if money matters have not been moved to the back burner. We get daily reminders that the reaper could knock at our door tomorrow and most of us would not want to be caught messing with money matters. Eighty is a time for more being as opposed to doing, marshaling our energy for mindfulness, deepening relationships, trying to do a little good somewhere, valuing our time.

Give some time to maximizing return. You know the no-free-lunch rule requires some attention: e.g., search for highest yield CDs; every other year consider concentrating your tax-deductible expenses (contributions, real estate taxes, etc.), paying them in January and December of the same calendar year and take the standard deduction in the following year; setting up your assets to transfer to your children upon death (TOD) to avoid probate. If you are sitting on a lot of cash, consider lending money to family members (for mortgages, student loans, car financing). You can beat the current rate they are paying while raising the rate you now receive (close to zero for CDs and money markets).

Don't get so concerned over whether you will have sufficient resources to get the care you may need at the end. There is not much you can do about it now. Remember that most of us competently die without a long stay in a nursing home.

The primary function of money should be the purchase of time. Don't get trapped into doing things you'd rather not, just because it pays. And do pay for freeing up time for the things you like to do.

Decide how much you are willing to give away for the year. (The biblical 10% is a good starting point.) Having done this makes writing the checks easy and for a year you can toss all solicitations without opening them.

Don't sweat the legacy bit. You should have trained your kids not to expect much. Don't tell them about former Treasury Secretary Paul O'Neill who had $330 million in stocks at the time of his confirmation proceedings. When he was encouraged to sell some to avoid conflicts of interest he groused. "It didn't have anything to do with me. It was about giving away my kids legacy." Poor kids.

Having your affairs in order is the nicest gift you can make to those cleaning up behind you. Go make up a folder containing a list of assets, insurance policies, credit cards, etc. Send the kids or whoever, an email telling them where to look for it.

Don't be afraid to spend money on something utterly frivolous. You don't need any help with this.

Marriage: The Good, the Bad and the Ugly

Several years ago, while sitting in the observation car of a train to Denali, Betty and I were joined by two women who appeared to be in their late 20s. After exchanging a few comments about the Alaskan landscape, one of them turned to Betty and asked how long we had been married.

Betty: "56 years."

With a bemused expression, the questioner said, "56. How does that work?"

Yes. How does that work?

Let's get a few stats on the table before moving on to more personal things. Marriage rates have plummeted to a 40-year low; half of all marriages end in divorce and those who stay married are said to be less happy than couples of the previous decade. Forty percent of married American men do not describe themselves as "very happy in this state." Young people are increasingly pessimistic about their chances for a lasting union, people are waiting longer to get married, one-third of the births in the U.S. are outside of marriage and there is a strong trend for marriage to be restricted to the well educated and more affluent, the group least likely to divorce.

Kent & Betty with their three daughters (left to right) Jill, Casey & Ann, Easter, 1962

A study called "The Gray Divorce Revolution" found that one in four people over 50 divorced in 2009, compared with one in ten in 1990. The number of dating site users over 50 is growing twice as fast as any other age group.

But wait. In the midst of all this skepticism and doubt, there is a yearning for a lasting relationship and the frequency of serial marriages surely reflects the dominance of hope over experience. A recent survey found married men to be happier than single, and a surprising three-fourths said that their sex life is better within marriage. While developing market strategies for Fortune 500 companies, investigators were surprised to learn that long-term marriage is a new status symbol.

Certainly, some people have terrible things happen that stress a marriage beyond repair: health problems, accidents, loss of a job, the death of a child, abuse, irreconcilable differences.

Marriage is hard. Even conservative Christians who call for a constitutional amendment to protect the institution are now acknowledging it is not easy. (The Pew Forum reports that evangelicals are more likely to be divorced than Roman Catholics, Mormons, Muslims, Jew, Hindus, and atheists.)

Researchers tell us that the following features are found in marriages that last: commitment, willingness to compromise, sense of humor, mutual respect, good communication, flexibility. Such saintly people must be in short supply, so if you find someone with these qualities, grab them.

Surveys reveal that luck is the primary reason offered by couples celebrating a golden anniversary, most claiming that the longer they are together, the luckier they feel. This is a modest stance but goes against the argument that only about 10 percent of life is entirely random. Psychologist Richard Wiseman (how could he be wrong with that surname?) argues that research reveals that "lucky" people are open to unexpected possibilities, listen to hunches, make good choices without knowing why and have a special ability to turn bad luck into good fortune.

If you have nothing else to go on, take as a model a couple sitting in front of me at a baseball game. The woman's shirt read: "I love you more today than yesterday. Yesterday you really got on my nerves." Or the woman who was asked if she had ever considered divorce:

"Divorce, no. Murder, yes." These two are not afraid to express an opinion and aren't expecting all peaches and cream.

A word of advice for anyone searching for a partner through a dating service or through the personals in the back of magazines. Which of these ads from Harvard Magazine would you respond to?

1 Smart, slender and very attractive, refreshingly authentic with lots of heart and an athletic passion for the outdoors...spontaneous and easygoing, curious with wonderful smile, lively humor and a touch of mischief...romantic at heart.

2 Santa Monica shrew, no particular virtues seeks curmudgeon 54+ for pointless liaison.

Which of these two would more likely be flexible, modest, willing to take a chance and have a sense of humor?

(More on this topic next time.)

Long-Term Marriages Need Glue

Following up on last week's column on long-term marriage, I focus here on a few of the things that "glue" couples together.

Touch each other. Marriage counselors tell us that non-sexual touching is crucial to a successful marriage, particularly for women. Surprisingly, the absence of such touching is listed as one of the top 10 reasons for divorce.

Stay away from pre-nuptial agreements (except for late-life marriages where the intent is to protect the children). Much of life is shaped by expectation and hope, and you don't want to muddy the water at the outset by codifying your reservations.

Pay attention to your mate. Make eye contact once in a while. When you say to your partner, "How did your day go?" actually listen to the response. If you notice for the first time that he is walking with a cane or she has a patch over one eye, make inquiry. If she asks you would you like to go to bed early, reflect on the question rather than assuming she is sleepy.

Bring into the marriage some stuff from the outside. Former Speaker of the House John McCormack and his wife Harriet had an unbroken string of 18,000 nights together in their burrow, during which John solicitously cut the meat on Harriett's plate. For recreation, they took solitary walks, seemingly sufficient for one another. This kind of closeness would act as a solvent for our marriage. Most of us need to be out and about. Sometimes together, sometimes with others. Yes, even at this advanced age we ought to be learning some new things. Bring in something to talk about other than how the government has gone to hell.

As always, not everybody buys into this. Take Sean Connery, who says that the secret to his 30-year marriage was that he and his wife did not have a shared language: "The inability to hold extended conversations—and to bicker—-is what has kept us together all these years."

Learn something new. A few days after our marriage, a time when fully-cooked breakfasts appeared every day on tables all across America, I was enjoying such a meal prepared by Betty when I idly warned her that I didn't know how to cook. A few minutes later, as I washed dishes, Betty dropped *The Joy of Cooking* on the counter, smiled sweetly and said, "You're a good reader." Sure enough, after the babies came, I cooked breakfast until the girls moved on, and just this morning I made Betty's oatmeal.

Come to an understanding about vacations. Betty has a move-on gene that calls for travel, new vistas, the viewing of alien peoples, churches, and gardens. I love the routine of being at home, going to work, messing around, sleeping in my own bed, watching "The Daily Show." So over the years with the approach of vacation and taking the children to visit grandparents, I tended to irritability, sciatica and skin rashes. But Betty gave me a life-changing insight when she explained that I was on vacation 50 weeks of the year and surely I could go on work for two weeks.

Learn something about conflict resolution. Experts have identified the five most common sources of conflict: money, sex, children, in-laws, household chores and leisure time. But we are told that the issues are not as important as how the conflict is resolved. Do some reading and if you feel the need for more glue, you could do worse than visiting a family mediator.

Learn to whistle. Don't laugh. Have you ever known a whistler who is not light-hearted, content, optimistic, good company? Imagine the tone that would be set if candidates running for office were required to whistle for three minutes before every debate. Imagine, if you can, Justices Scalia and Thomas whistling softly as they enter the courtroom. Now transfer this to marital disagreements. (Caveat: stay away from the likes of Ludwig Wittgenstein, who could whistle the solo part of an entire concerto while a pianist played the orchestral part. You would not want to be tied up with someone that competent or that much of a show-off.) Work on a duet.

Monday, February 10, 2014

Ageism Is a Continuing Problem

We like pretty people. Research confirms what we know intuitively: good things happen to the good looking. They earn more money, get promoted more often and are more likely to get married. Obese women earn 17 percent less than non-obese; tall men earn more, each additional inch in height is worth a 2.7 percent increase in income. One-third of CEOs are 6-foot-2, while the average American male is 5-foot-9. (About that height thing. I recently asked my orthopedic surgeon friend how much height I might have lost by age 86: "Oh, about three or four inches.")

Now keep all of this in mind as we focus on the following picture:

Curved back. Bald head. Stooped shoulders. White beard. Lined face. The startling reflection coming to me from the shop window reminded me of my father when he was in his 90s. I am not only old, but get daily evidence that I look it.

Betty reminds me to hold my shoulders back (OK, at my request). My son-in-law suggests that I swing my arms as I walk, knowing that not swinging them is an early symptom of Parkinson's. If I am sitting on the floor and someone enters the room, they rush over to help, assuming that I must have fallen, and ask in a loud voice, "Can you hear me?"

The grocery store checkout counter provides a searing picture of the way the young see me. The 30-year-old cashier greets me with a gratuitous reference to my age — "How are you today, young man?" — not realizing that he is being patronizing. The bagger wants to know if the third item she is putting in the bag will make it too heavy for me. The cashier watches, expecting me to have trouble in swiping the credit card. I have to wrestle the grocery cart away from the young man who assumes that I could never make it to the car on my own. All three are courteous and helpful, but embrace the common perspective that anyone who looks as I do is close to the end and needs help.

(Who knows, maybe one of these people had helped a friend of ours by pushing her grocery cart through a packed parking lot in search of her car. Finding the car after 10 minutes of cruising up and down the rows, the man said, "Lady, it would have helped if you had told there was a canoe on top.")

Yes, most of us have lost a number of steps but are not yet the senile, physically dependent, overly demanding, unproductive old geezers that we appear to be. We have made considerable progress on racism and sexism, but ageism is another thing. The physical changes with age translate to an expectation of mental decline also, of inevitable decay in all dimensions. All too often the expectation is fulfilled. But not always. Which is the point.

There is not a lot to be done about that "not pretty" business. It will cost you in terms of being invisible, ignored, exposed to condescension. Don't sweat it; it will not be personal and you will have a lot of company. But you don't have to roll over. Some fun can come from letting others know that you have a fix on what is going down. You might emulate Edgar Comee, recently of Brunswick, Maine. For situations in which he was treated as a child, he passed out a small card that reads, "Use of first names by younger persons in dealing with the elderly is presumptuous, demeaning, disrespectful and condescending, as though the offender were speaking to a child in need of guidance, correction or possibly a pat on the head and/or bottom."

We will be busy fighting ageism for a while to come.

At some point you are going to need some help and you should take it when offered, even if you might not have put much in the bank of good deeds.

Confession: I have known some really boring octogenarians. If in a public place and having a choice of sitting next to someone who looks like me and someone of another generation, I would take the other generation.

Sleep Isn't as Simple as It Seems

Virginia Tech history professor, Roger Ekirch, says that it was standard for our ancestors to sleep in two sessions: one of three or four hours followed by wakefulness of two to three hours before sleeping again. The time between "first" and "second" sleep was typically used for reading, conversing, contemplation, prayer, sex. But this was yesterday, a less complex and hectic time.

In the early '90s, Thomas Wehr of the National Institutes of Mental Health conducted an interesting study of the effect of light on sleep patterns. His subjects spent four weeks with restricted daylight, staying up 10 hours (instead of the usual 16). The rest of the time they were in a closed, dark room where they were to sleep or rest as much as possible. They began to sleep four or five hours and wake for several hours before sleeping again. The time between the two sleeps was characterized by unusual calmness likened to meditation. For our purposes here, the point is that there is more than one way of doing things. The next time you wake at 2 a.m. and can not get back to sleep, just remember you are replicating the behavior of grandparents of some generations ago.

The inability to get a good night's sleep is now a national concern. Note that every city of any size is graced with a sleep disorder center and the following numbers reflect its extensivity. Polls find that 25 percent of adults had trouble sleeping the prior day. One in 25 admitted falling asleep while driving in the previous month and 15 to 33 percent of all fatal crashes in the U.S. might involve a drowsy driver. Studies show that two weeks of sleeping only 6 hours a night can have the same impact as one or two nights of total deprivation. The number of "short sleepers" (less than six hours) is on the rise.

The picture is even bleaker for the elderly, with 50 percent complaining of chronic trouble with sleep, spending more time in bed, but getting less. Sleep patterns are disrupted by major life changes (loss of a spouse, changed living arrangements), side effects of medications, chronic diseases, etc.

It's hard not to be anxious. The National Sleep Foundation tells us that adults need 7 to 9 hours of sleep each night. We are reminded of all the good things that happen with good sleep: It allows the body to repair itself, refreshes the immune system and prevents disease. Insufficient sleep results in increased morbidity and mortality, deficits in attention and short-term memory and depression. *The Wall Street Journal* reports that 29 percent of workers have fallen asleep or been very sleepy on the job, resulting in a significant impact on the gross domestic product.

Oh, one other thing to work into your schedule: two hours of sunlight each day to compensate for the fact that your aging body is not producing enough of the hormone melatonin.

Relax. Take a deep breath. Once again, we are not all alike and sleep needs vary from person to person. And there is disagreement over simple questions like whether older people need less sleep. Come back to this column next week for specific actions that can make a difference. Meanwhile, if you are having trouble sleeping, you might try reading this column three times.

Sunday, February 23, 2014

Here's How to Get a Good Night's Sleep

Last week I promised some tips on controlling your sleep problems. Here, in the first few paragraphs, is the meat of what the experts offer:

Environment: Use the bed only for sex and sleep. Cut off all electronic devices, especially smartphones. Avoid light, noise and extremes in temperature in the bedroom. Get some sunshine (for melatonin).

Diet: Late in the day, limit caffeine, big meals, and spicy food. Go easy on the alcohol and consider eating a light snack before bedtime.

Miscellaneous: Exercise during the day, as it releases endorphins and all kinds of good stuff.

Take sleeping medications rarely, if at all. Avoid all advice coming from someone who tells you to reduce the stress and anxiety in your life as if you had control over it. Avoid napping late in the day. Strive to get in and out of bed about the same time every day. Establish some bedtime rituals that help with the transition between wakefulness and drowsiness, e.g., warm bath, listening to music, reading for 10 minutes.

You know all of this. Just go do it. And keep in mind that the number of hours you sleep is not the crucial factor. The important variable is how you feel.

Would you be interested in an activity that improves learning, memory and overall health, in one hour can improve alertness for up to ten hours, requires no new equipment and only limited training, can take place almost anywhere, has few negative side effects and is free? Yes. I thought so.

It's napping. Our great-granddaughter, Olivia, just turning two, visited us this week. She was being read to when she put her hand on the book and said, "Stop." When asked if she wanted to get into her bed, she nodded yes. Smart girl. I was ready to join her. We are competent nappers and we fit the stereotype that naps are for the two extremes of the age spectrum. Others of different ages who indulge are seen as lazy or lacking in ambition.

However, the Pew Research Center has generated some interesting stats. It says about a third of us say we napped the previous day with the number bouncing to 50% of those over age eighty.

A number of famous people have embraced habitual siestas lasting from five minutes to three hours—google "famous nappers, the art of manliness." Winston Churchill's routine included daily two-hour naps; he kept a bed in the Houses of Parliament saying that the sleep enabled him to get twice as much done each day.

Lyndon Johnson napped daily for thirty minutes encouraged by Jackie Kennedy, who said, "It changed Jack's whole life." Napoleon could drop to sleep immediately even with cannons firing nearby. Thomas Edison bragged about how hard he worked, how he slept only a few hours a night. But an assistant pointed out that it was not unusual for Edison to insert two three-hour naps during the day. Nancy Reagan denied that Ronald was a napper, but his diaries proved otherwise. Upon leaving office, he suggested his chair be engraved with "Ronald Reagan Slept Here."

As you embrace napping, you need to keep in mind that the process is as much art as science and you have to work at learning what works for you. For example, a 10 to 20-minute nap might do to get you back to work. For cognitive memory processing, a 60-minute nap may do more. A ninety-minute nap will involve a full cycle of sleep which adds creativity, emotional and procedural memory. But if you want to sleep at night, avoid napping late in the day.

There is a lot more to say on this topic, but sorry, it's time for some zzzzzzzzzzz.

Forgiveness Has Many Benefits to the Giver

Within a two week period, three unconnected people suggested that I write about forgiveness. This could be about 30% of my readership, so here it is.

For most of us, any consideration of forgiveness is likely to be in the familiar context of religion and the church. We are talking here about a voluntary process in which the forgiver lets go of negative emotions such as the desire for revenge or has a decreased desire to wish the offender ill. It does not mean forgetting or excusing an offense. The hope is that the process not only gets past the negative but results in an increase in positive emotions.

In recent years, social scientists and medical professionals have taken an interest in the subject and this is the primary focus of my comments.

Even a superficial search on the internet yields surprising (to me) evidence of widespread attention to forgiveness. Stanford University has a research center devoted to it and for $250 you can attend a four-session workshop on forgiveness with objectives such as:

explaining or managing anger and hurt; describing the advantages to forgiveness as a general problem-solving strategy. Researchers are validating and quantifying their studies with the help of recent advances in brain imaging and blood chemistry.

Forgiveness is not easy and takes time. And some offenses are so heinous, e.g., murder of a family member, that forgiveness can't be reached. But some have succeeded even here. And you shouldn't be hard on yourself if you can't get to total forgiveness.

Unforgiveness can take a heavy toll. Hope College psychologist Charlotte Witvliet asked people to think of someone who had offended them while she monitored their blood pressure, heart rate, facial muscle tension, and sweat gland activity. All of these measures soared. When she asked her subjects to try to empathize with her offender or imagine forgiveness, the physical arousal coasted downward.

The following observations seem to have some empirical foundation.

* Forgiveness has a strong positive impact on mental health, physical symptoms, medications, sleep, fatigue, somatic complaints. These benefits seem to increase with age. Positive emotions towards a transgressor result in lowered blood pressure, the release of hormones that help fight infection and a variety of other good results.

* By and large, the benefits of forgiveness go to the giver rather than the offender.

* It not only restores positive thoughts, feelings, and behaviors toward the offender, but it spills over into the same for others not in the relationship.

* If you are dead set on wronging someone and hope to be forgiven, you could do worse than choosing an older woman who believes

that she has been forgiven by some higher power (age, gender, belief, all three are correlated with a willingness to forgive).

- It does not require face-to-face contact with the person offended.

- Forgiveness is positively correlated with volunteerism, donating to charity, and other altruistic behaviors.

We are in the early stages of understanding all of this, but a scientific structure is evolving. There is enough here to make me consider taking out an ad in the *Democrat* in which I would forgive all those people who have offended me over the years. Anybody like to share the cost of a full-page ad?

Humor Helps Cope with Grief

Columnist Leonard Pitts reminds us of what we know intuitively. We laugh to keep from crying (*Democrat* 3/10/14). To illustrate the point he notes the path that comedian Laurie Kilmartin took as she tweeted about her father's dying, quickly gathering 42,000 followers of her jokes and grief.

In last week's column, I wrote about some of the positive benefits of forgiveness. Researchers have reported similar therapeutic effects with humor: e.g., improvement in the functioning of immune and central nervous systems; help in coping with stress and pain of everyday tasks.

The understanding of humor evolves over a lifetime and is determined by cognitive, verbal, and social abilities. Recent research has focused on the development of neural systems and the importance of the prefrontal cortex, a process aided by fMRI studies. (This is the decade for neurologists, as we focus on the brain for an understanding of all behavior. In Doctorow's latest book, *Andrew's Brain,* the main character is a cognitive scientist.)

The professionals divide humor into two elements: *cognitive* refers to understanding the joke, comprehending the disparities between the punch line and prior experience; the *affective* element involves enjoying the joke, producing visceral and emotional responses, depending upon the hilarity. Who would have thought that a simple joke could lead to all of this? And I won't bore you with sentences such as this: "The volume of the frontal cortex and its pronounced age-related alterations in the 5-HT2 and D2 receptor availability... point to the impairment of executive functions including working memory, inhibition, and planning." Oops. I did bore you.

The research on humor with elderly populations is limited. What there is suggests that in comparison with younger adults they enjoy humor more, like aggressive humor less, have increasing difficulties in understanding jokes. Coming across a statement that the elderly are especially offended by jokes referring to old age, gave me pause. The writer has not seen my inbox full of such jokes sent by my peers.

Grief can be so overwhelming as to immobilize. Its nature was caught so well in a letter written by the Queen Mother after the death of her husband, George VI: "It was a day when one felt engulfed by great black clouds of unhappiness and misery.... How small and selfish is sorrow.... It bangs one about until one is senseless."

In this context, humor can give us some perspective, some assistance in getting out from under the clouds. So, I end with a joke or two.

A wife calls the lab to get her husband's test results and was told there had been a mix up because of identical names and they could not sort it out. The diagnosis for one was Alzheimer's and AIDS for the other. The wife wanted to know what to do. After a pause she was told to leave her husband in the city and if he returned home, not to have sex with him.

And a favorite of mine, reinforced just this week: A man was asked what words he would like spoken over his casket. He replied, "Look, he's moving!" Workers at a Mississippi funeral home were shocked when a corpse started moving in a body bag. Walter Williams, age

78, about to be embalmed, was pulled out and taken to a hospital. His daughter said her father couldn't remember any of it, he was just asleep (noted in *The Week*).

Sunday, March 23, 2014

We Do Not Need Work to Define Us

In my first week in a doctoral program at the University of Texas (1951), a handout given to me produced considerable anxiety. E.G. Boring (yes), the author of the classic history of psychology, listed the following requirements for success as a psychologist: must be single; expect to put in 80-90 hours per week; should not be distracted by other work; excited about the weekend because he could be in the lab without interfering events that come during the week.

Reading the paper, I kept looking for a reference to April Fools or some such. Not finding anything, I knew there was trouble ahead since I was married to a feminist (before I even knew that word existed) who was pregnant and I had never worked 80 hours a month, much less a week.

But being a product of the hardest working nation in the industrialized world, I sucked it up and went to work.

Now jump ahead over the 24 years that I have been fully retired. For most of us, our work has been the defining feature of our lives. In addition to providing the wherewithal, it structures our days, impacts our self-perceptions, meets our social needs and much more. We take pride in being hard workers and readily tell anybody who will listen how busy we are. And it is not by chance that when meeting someone for the first time a common question is, *What do you do?* Never mind that a recent survey found that we waste two hours of our working day, not counting lunch and scheduled breaks. Even Einstein was known to be a first-class loafer on his job as a clerk. It is said that as he daydreamed while watching a builder on a nearby rooftop, he came up with the theory of relativity.

For all these reasons, retirement or loss of a job can present serious problems. I recall Simone de Beauvoir's description of a depressed elderly Frenchman who had been forced to retire after a lifetime of work with the subway system. "I was a ticket taker," he declared. Now he was nothing. Some of my professor colleagues have had similar feelings, but they can at least pretend to be writing a history of the department or some such.

But retirement offers possibilities not previously on the table. Most of us need work, but with an expanded definition. One that involves being in community, having a place that expects you to show up, of contributing to a better world. One that takes advantage of the skills and knowledge accumulated over time. (Note: A shameful proportion of our people can never dream of retirement because they live in poverty, struggling to survive. Just this week there was a report that 37% have saved less than $1000 for retirement.)

There is merit in periodically auditing how you are spending the leisure time you control (that which is left over from taking care of the body). It is here that our truest priorities may be found.

But as you audit, keep in mind how much sand is in the bottom of the glass. If you are ever going to search for fun and laughter it should be now. Heed Samuel Butler: "All animals, except man, know that the principal business of life is to enjoy it."

Are People Helping or Just Showing Microaggression?

As I stepped into the street I saw two women about a block away walking toward me and decided to show them what a power walk looks like. But after a few minutes, I realized I was now hearing their voices and I was the one getting a demonstration of serious walking. When they were a few feet away, one of them said, "Your shoe is untied. Can I tie it for you?"

Later in the morning, I was wandering around in the hospital in search of the Neuroscience Center when a doctor in scrubs joined me in the elevator. Upon my inquiring, he gave me directions but also escorted me.

Several hours later when I stepped into the parking garage, I paused to recall where I had parked the car. Immediately a security officer came over to ask if he could help with anything. No, I was ok, just remembering which level I was on. He asked for my car keys, started walking, pressed the panic button, setting off the horn and flashing lights.

These three incidents in close succession didn't do much for my self-perception as an Alpha Male. I tied my own shoe and I would have found the center and car. But it is possible that these three people committed a microaggression. (It was not in my vocabulary either until three days ago.)

Derald Sue, a professor at Columbia University, author of two books on the subject, says a microaggression is "an everyday verbal or behavioral slight, put down, indignity...unintentionally directed toward a marginalized group such as race, gender, sexual orientation." I would add the elderly and as an example, I cite the store cashier mentioned in an earlier column, who greeted me with "How are you today young man?"

Sue says that microaggression has become one of the most researched areas in the literature of psychology. He advocates using education to help people explore their unconscious biases and nip them in the bud before they develop.

Now back to the three helpers I mentioned above. Were they displaying an unconscious bias against the elderly in assuming that I needed help on the basis of my advanced age? Possibly. But I was not offended and am inclined to take it for what it appeared to be—people helping someone they perceived to be in need.

The grocery store cashier was more clearly committing a microaggression and it might be helpful for him to know it. But simply calling him out will not do the job, as he is not likely to know what you are talking about. Any success here will come only after a long-term educational effort, made difficult by the fact that we are dealing with subtle distinctions and unconscious biases.

But there is something that we can work on immediately. Our current political and social climate seems to be saturated with angry voices and division. It wouldn't hurt us to lighten up, take off the hair shirt, cut one another a little slack.

I'm willing to take my three helpers I mentioned above at face value, just good, caring people. Besides, if we can hang in a while longer and the trending age structure of the population holds, the sheer number of us old ones will put us in control.

Sunday, April 6, 2014

It's Never Too Late to Start Training Your Brain

As I opened up the computer, an ad managed to get through the filters and pop up on the screen: challenge your brain with scientifically-designed training. In the company of 50 million members from 182 countries, the reader is encouraged to sign up for a personalized program focused on improving memory and attention.

By now you know how crucial physical exercise is for your health. You may not act on it, but know that you should. A goodly number of readers of this column go to gyms, have personal trainers or own exercise equipment. Some of you have even quit complaining about it (yes, I'm with you).

But that was yesterday. Today's focus is on that three-pound hunk of meat known as the brain and the neurologists who are messing around with it.

The neurologists are riding high, aided by technological advances. They are teasing out the functions of specific neural wiring for all kinds of behaviors. The understanding is that, contrary to earlier thinking, we are not hard-wired at birth. The brain is plastic, subject to structural change by external events, even in advanced age.

Specific areas of the brain have been shown to expand or constrict in size depending on usage, not unlike muscular growth through physical exercise. Merely thinking about something can alter brain function.

So how do we go about cognitive training? Not to worry. There are lots of people with suggestions in this following sample of recent books: *Train Your Mind, Change Your Brain*; *Smarter: The New Science of Building Brain Power;* and *The Future of the Mind: The Scientific Quest to Understand, Enhance, and Empower the Mind.*

My superficial reading on this subject leaves me intrigued about the possibilities of change this late in life. But we are still in the early stages of building a scientific underpinning. For example, there are differing opinions on the value of repetitive practice with crossword puzzles and various computer games, as compared with taking on entirely new ventures. If you have mastered a specific challenge, it will take less attention than would new activities. Without much to go on, I would vote for new ventures—bird watching, dancing lessons, skydiving, bonsai, bridge, photography, anything new.

While working on this column I received an email from a friend who was excited about a TED Talk by neuroscientist Daniel Reisel, who studied the brains and behavior of psychopaths in prisons and rats in the lab. His findings led him to conclude that an impoverished environment leads to an underdeveloped amygdala (a mass of gray matter in the temporal lobe).

An enriched social environment can lead the brain to generate new neurons—under the right conditions behavioral change is possible.

Sunday, April 13, 2014

The Power of the Necktie Is Waning

October, 1955. Dressing for my first day at work on a new job in Tallahassee, I put on a shirt, tie, and jacket. As I did five days a week for the better part of eight years. Without giving it a thought, I was making my contribution to the growth of a necktie industry worth $1.5 billion by 1995. Who would have thought that men by the millions, day after day, could be persuaded to wear a piece of cloth pulled tightly around their neck? For no obvious reason. Aside from being ornamental, a means of marking special occasions, a symbol of power and significance.

The history of the necktie reaches back hundreds of years, but not much of anything stays in place forever. Note these indications of change in the air. The $1.5 billion mentioned above has been cut in half. The *Men's Dress Furnishings Association*, the primary representative of tie manufacturers, has folded its tent. Quips like this can be heard: "What do you call a restaurant that requires a coat and tie? Empty."

Republicans chided Obama when he appeared in public tieless but had to back off when the people liked it or didn't seem to care. Other leaders, including conservative Vice-President candidate Paul Ryan, appeared in public sans tie. Same for The G8 world leaders: Cameron, Putin, etc. (Can someone tell me why basketball coaches wear ties?)

We can speculate about some of the forces behind this movement. Society is generally more casual. We used to dress up when flying. If my mother could see what deplaning passengers are wearing (or not wearing), she would be astounded. The young internet entrepreneurs, making it without climbing the traditional corporate ladder, would not be caught dead in suit and tie.

A more significant argument for ditching the tie resides in research reported in prestigious medical journals. The primary problem is that ties constrict the free flow of oxygenated blood to the brain and sensory organs of the head, leading to high blood pressure, damage to the optic nerve, false diagnoses, possibly leading to glaucoma. Typical of the research is that of Susan Watkins, who studied 94 men. She found that 67% were buying shirts with a neck size smaller than the circumference of their necks, invoking some of the problems mentioned above. A simple guideline is that you should be able to slide the index finger between the neck and the collar.

(While researching the tie issues, I came across an article in the *Archives of Internal Medicine* titled "The Tight Pants Syndrome". It involves remarkable parallels with the necktie.)

If you are in the elderly category you don't need the excuse of health issues, the evolving power of no-tie, or some difficulty in making a knot, in order to ditch the tie. Just do it. Most people will cut you a little slack.

I am close to a trip to Goodwill with my handful of ties, but not 100% there. This summer we will be traveling across the country for two weddings and if any of the significant players indicate they would like for me to put on a tie, I certainly will. Two hours of torture is a low cost for a lifetime of love. And I take some consolation in knowing that future generations will look back in amusement at one of our sillier customs.

You Think You Have Memory Problems

There are a lot of people who want you to "just relax," "be aware of what is going on around you," "let your troubles fall away," "live in the moment." Help in doing this is readily available through a variety of books, workshops, videos, accompanied by testimonials to life-changing experiences.

So today I bring you Henry Molaison, the ultimate *live in the moment* person. At age 10 he suffered from severe epilepsy, with frequent grand mal seizures. At age 27, he underwent experimental surgery which involved the removal of pieces of his brain (or, if you prefer, bilateral medial temporal lobe resection). The result? The seizures were controlled but at the cost of a catastrophic amnesia.

Psychologist Suzanne Corkin tells his story in her 2013 book *Permanent Present Tense*. You think you have memory problems? Forgeddaboutit. Molaison (known as H.M. to protect his privacy) would have gladly swapped conditions. His memory bank was restricted to events prior to the surgery, and he was unable to add to the bank. Any experience more than a moment long slips out the back door. Corkin studied H.M. for over 30 years but when she walks into a room and asks H.M. if they have met before, he replies, "I think we have." Asked where, H.M. answers, "Maybe in high school." He cannot remember a meal he has just eaten or a picture he has just seen.

He could play bingo, repeat a string of numbers (in the absence of an intervening event), complete crossword puzzles, do simple arithmetic in his head. He was said to be pleasant, engaging, and had a sense of humor.

H.M. was an agreeable subject for a multitude of researchers right up until his death in 2008, making possible significant advances in our understanding of the way memory works (google his name and get over 60,000 hits). Here are just a few of the conclusions that came out of his cooperation as a subject.

- The surgery he received should not be repeated on anyone.

- Memory is not one spot in the brain.

- There are different kinds of memory, involving different processes, each with its own biological foundation.

- All sensory modes (sight, sound, touch, smell, taste), contribute to memory.

- Various kinds of memory operate outside of conscious awareness.

H.M. will continue to contribute to our understanding of memory through the study of his brain. It has been cut into 2,401 slices, put into a preservative solution, and frozen. Studies of these slides will reveal information about what kind of dementia he had, the organizations and connections of neurons, and much more. The basic question is how do physical changes in the brain contribute to cognitive loss?

It is well known that an 80-year-old brain is dramatically different from that of a 20 year old, particularly with respect to total volume. As I write this, I am amazed anew that my 86-year-old gray matter can store and bring into the present my memory of 83 years ago when my mother dressed me to represent the New Year, pulling a red wagon full of presents.

How does that work?

Neuroscientists would love to be able to answer that question. They are encouraged by recent technical advances that allow better mapping of the 100 trillion connections that constitute the brain's neural networks. According to Corkin, the goal is to understand how the billions of neurons, each with 10,000 synapses, interact to create the mind. Wish them great good luck. (Don't worry about the numbers above. They are the best I could find. And no, I don't know how they are counting.)

But this research, along with work on Alzheimer's and other forms of dementia, may give some hope to baby boomers and future generations.

Generation Gap Larger than Ever

I have been thinking lately about the kind of world that our generation will be passing on to our grandchildren — global warming, constant wars and violence of every kind, concern about water supplies, rapidly expanding inequality. It's enough to bring to mind the old curse, "May you live in interesting times." If we are not yet there, we certainly have reason to be uneasy about what may be around the corner.

Sam, our youngest grandchild, is 19 and a sophomore in college. He is also a member of the latest generation, the Millennials. (If this is the first time you have registered this word, don't feel badly. As with it as I am, it is only recently that I learned about selfies.)

At 86, I can't pretend to know what Sam thinks about (with one or two exceptions). But thanks to the Pew Research Center and the Gallup poll, we know a lot about the Millennials, 50 million strong, who were born between 1984-2004. And I know a little about the Greatest Generation (saved the world) and the Silent Generation (conformist and civic). I focus here on these three, skipping over the Baby Boomers and Gen Xers.

The Millennials have fewer attachments to traditional political and religious institutions, but they pray. They are set apart by singlehood, with only one in four married, although one in three has a child. One in eight lives with a parent, with one in three unemployed. They are the most highly educated generation, carrying a heavy education debt. In the face of all these problems, they remain optimistic.

They constitute by far the most racially diverse group ever, with 43 percent non-white. An active government is favored for solving problems (except when it comes to personal choices). They are civic-minded, want to do good, and keep Social Security and Medicare for their parents. (More than half believe there will be no money for their Social Security.) And finally, make what you can out of the fact that four in 10 have at least one tattoo and/or body piercing. (Please tell me how they can be that masochistic and irrational.)

Critics of the Millennials see them as feeling entitled, whiners spoiled by their parents, embracing a "What, me worry?" attitude.

Even from this necessarily sketchy picture, it is not surprising that the gap between the Millennials and their elders is the largest ever and the political implications are significant. On the following issues, the Millennials take a significantly more liberal position: same-sex marriage, legalization of marijuana, immigration, the role of government. Their views on gun control and abortion are fairly close to that of their elders.

Reports from Gallup just two months ago were titled "Seniors Have Realigned With the Republican Party" and "Young Americans' Affinity for Democratic Party Has Grown." Columnist Charles Blow points out that until recently, much of the time the voting patterns of the young and elderly looked virtually identical. Since 2004 in presidential elections, the share of the vote of young Americans has increased and the share of older Americans has fallen.

Young voters went strongly for Obama in 2008, but they have been disappointed with him lately. According to a poll of Millennials by the Harvard Institute of Politics, they are also disappointed by government in general and particularly the gridlock in Congress. They self-identify as Independent and vote Democratic.

Now, back to the kind of world we are leaving grandson Sam. I am encouraged by the Millennials. They just might get it together and make some progress. They embrace the notion of doing good, remain optimistic in the face of adversity, do not have an extreme agenda and advocate policies that coincide with my own. Stay tuned. Things can quickly change.

Sunday, May 18, 2014

Unmarried Couples Face a Variety of Legal Issues

Continuing my thoughts about our grandchildren (the Millennials), I reminisced about my own courtship. The radical change in sexual mores over 60 years was brought about in large part by the advent of "The Pill," which made family planning more a matter of choice than chance.

In 1950, when we were married, the norm for our slice of middle-class life was to go to college, marry, get a job, have a family. Betty and I conformed to that pattern. We married and three days later we had moved to Columbus, Mo., found an apartment, a job for Betty as a counselor at Stephens College, graduate school for Kent. A little later we bought a 1938 Plymouth for $162.50 (the 50 cents came from splitting the difference between our offer of $150 and the asking price of $175) and had our first child before our second anniversary.

My, how things do change. When we were at William and Mary we never knew of a single instance where a couple lived together outside of marriage. Today the estimate of unmarried couples living together is around 8 million (16 million people), 40 percent with children.

The trend among the Millennials to postpone marriage could provoke some interesting discussion, but my focus at the moment is on the need to pay attention to the legal consequences associated with not being married.

For some guidance, I sat down with a family lawyer, a longtime friend. She easily ticked off things that could go badly wrong, since the special rules that govern married couples (i.e. property ownership, divorce, inheritance) do not exist outside of marriage. The following sample of legal problems should be getting the attention of our grandchildren, but doesn't. This is understandable since at their age they are immortal and couldn't possibly focus on consequences so far in the future.

In the unmarried state you lose out on tax advantages, Social Security, pension benefits and some benefits for dependent children; health insurance under a spouse's program; the right to stay in the home after a breakup; the right to maintenance support following a breakup; the right to visit your partner in the hospital or make medical decisions on their behalf. And a long list of other things if children are involved.

My lawyer friend explained that there are ways of heading off some of these problems ahead of time through legal documents and informal agreements. Information is readily available on the internet, ranging from suggestions about the handling of credit cards to various legal documents. A few hours of reading or with a family lawyer might avoid loads of stress.

My friend pointed out that late-life unmarried couples (also increasing in frequency) contain a different, but important set of potential problems, particularly concerning end-of-life decisions. As for late-life marriages where each spouse has a different set of children, there are potential problems of inheritance and property distribution.

I would encourage any couple entering into a late-life marriage to meet with a lawyer.

Having said all of this, the essential idea behind marriage remains unchanged. It is the need to love and be loved, to belong. It is the idea of commitment, faithfulness, loyalty, wanting the best for someone else.

Sunday, May 25, 2014

The Body Affects the Mind and Vice Versa

Once again we old people have done favors for certain segments of the community. By hanging around so long in such big numbers, thereby increasing the incidence of Parkinson's, other degenerative diseases and depression, we have boosted the outlook for the relatively recent specialty of neurology and psychological neurology.

The predictions are that the demand will outrun the supply for decades. You might alert your grandchildren who are considering graduate study to keep this in mind. (At least some of the money would stay with the family.) Thanks in part to technical advances in imaging (e.g., fMRI) researchers are slicing and dicing the brain, literally in some instances, zeroing in on very minute areas and functions not possible until now. For the most part, the focus has been on the impact of the brain on behavior. But we now know that the street runs in both directions. What we think, can impact the structure and function of that three pounds of meat. (Sorry, that is what it is.)

The mind/body relationship continues to amaze me. Some years ago I came across an experiment that involved a subject being told to imagine that they had just eaten a particular food, an orange for example, and a few minutes later an analysis of their stomachs revealed the presence of the appropriate enzymes to digest an orange. Now I don't know anything about the quality of the research, or whether that particular experiment was replicated, but there can be no doubt about the impact of thoughts on bodily function, and the role of expectation.

Look at the impact of placebos in the medical world. Everybody reading this column likely has some notion about "sugar pills" (pills containing inert substances such as sugar, cornstarch, etc.) that are portrayed as helpful for particular problems. Any positive relief is due to the powers of suggestion or conventional conditioning which involves the association of a stimulus with a particular effect. You may be less familiar with nocebos, situations in which the actions are expected to get worse rather than better, and they do.

Present a placebo as a muscle relaxer and it has that effect. Present it as a tensor and it functions as such. Present a placebo as alcohol and some subjects will become intoxicated and demonstrate impairment. Decaffeinated coffee, presented as caffeinated, can evoke the effects associated with caffeinated.

There is a substantial list of studies such as these, all confirming the role of expectation. Interest in the placebo has steadily grown and there is now a sizable attempt to understand the mechanisms involved. Surveys suggest that about half of medical doctors have prescribed them at some time.

With older populations. attention has been focused on Parkinson's, depression, and anxiety disorders. Placebos have many advantages, including being cheap and avoiding the side effects associated with nearly all drugs. Along the way, we have learned, to no one's surprise, that the demeanor of the prescriber and the nature of the doctor/patient relationship are also crucial elements.

Of course, there are some downsides. Some critics hold that the success of the placebos has been overblown, that solid evidence is still out. Others are concerned about ethical issues, including the deception involved.

For me, at this time, the trade-offs balance out on the positive aspects of placebos. With the caveat that we keep funding research trying to understand exactly how the mind works.

When Should We Give Up the Car Keys?

Listening to some people talk — especially those under age 50 — you would think that getting us older drivers off the road ranks in importance just behind the search for world peace. A number of people have asked me to write on this subject, and yes, some of us should have quit driving some time ago.

We have already backed off driving at night, on the Interstate highways, around Boston, in bad weather, if we haven't had our coffee. But before giving in altogether, I encourage you to come along with me in considering a few background facts.

A 48-year old driver may be dangerous; an 88-year driver may be just fine. Ability, not age, rules.

From 65 to 70, accident rates are similar to middle-aged drivers.

Older drivers have this working for them: less likely to drive drunk, speed, text while driving.

Beginning at age 75, fatal crash rates increase and rise sharply after age 80. (In part because old people are fragile and less likely to survive crashes.) Teenagers kill others, older drivers kill themselves.

None of these stats are of particular value to us as individuals, but they provide a background for issues that follow.

The cliché that the best defense is a good offense applies here, and you shouldn't be reluctant to initiate a conversation about old drivers. Inspect the cars of your children and grandchildren and inquire as to how those dents and scratches were acquired. Drop into conversation the fact that you have had only one ticket and just a few fender benders in 72 years on the road (yes, 72 — in Virginia a full driver's license could be had at age 14).

Tell them about the article you just read about boomers giving up driving for a few days as a means of sensitizing themselves to the loss of freedom. Wonder out loud about who would pick up the slack if you give up the keys. Is it possible to find a reliable taxi driver to call on? Maybe you can give the 1997 Grand Marquis to a grandchild or neighborhood kid in exchange for chauffeuring you around some? (The car might even be camp by now.) After all, having a driver would be the ultimate freedom.

Having done all of this, go read the National Highway Traffic Safety Administration five-year safety plan for older drivers, published in 2013. Focus on the behavior section, which emphasizes age-related functional changes such as strength, vision, flexibility, and cognition. Then go to the website of the American Occupational Therapy Association, which has a special program for the older driver, and where you can search by ZIP code for a therapist who specializes in driving rehabilitation.

Technological developments to make driving safer are rapidly expanding. Currently, cars with crash-avoidance systems are available on a number of models and soon we will be able to purchase cars that drive themselves. But we are not there yet.

Finally, listen to your children and others when they express concern about your driving. They care about you, otherwise they would be happy to have you continue to drive. If you think that you are a competent driver you should be willing to prove it by being evaluated by a third party. Do it.

Meanwhile, remember the turn signal and resist giving the finger to the horn-blowing driver behind you.

Friday, June 6, 2014

Having a 'Sense of Purpose' May Lengthen Life

My grandparents had 12 children, 10 of them girls. My image of Grandfather Rose is that of a rather stern man, and it is easy to believe the stories about suitors who called on Sunday afternoons. After a few visits, he would inquire about their intentions.

All of which is irrelevant except for bringing me to today's lesson, which is all about intention, finding a sense of purpose, having goals. I don't think it would be too much of a stretch to conclude that my grandparents found their goal in raising that brood. Both lived into their 90s.

Several major research projects reveal that having a sense of purpose leads to better health and longer life. These findings make for good headlines, and columnists —always on the lookout for subjects to write about — have jumped on the topic, thereby rapidly expanding exposure to the findings. Possibly beyond what is merited.

To give you a feel for the research I make brief reference to three recent studies.

In an article in *Psychological Science*, Patrick Hill and Nicholas Turiano describe their findings based on an analysis of the lives of over 7,000 adults aged 20 to 75, over a 14-year period. The authors organized the "sense of purpose" into four categories: creative, occupational or financial, prosocial, family oriented. A sense of purpose could come from improving social structure, helping people, raising children, climbing the corporate structure. They found that the people who died (549) were less likely to have had a sense of purpose.

A related study, *The Longevity Project,* came out of the University of California, Riverside, and was focused on 1,500 bright kids who were followed for decades. To their surprise, participants who were the most cheerful and had the best sense of humor lived shorter lives. The strongest health benefit came from being involved with and helping others. The most prudent and persistent were the healthiest. The "don't work too hard, don't stress yourself" attitude doesn't work for good health and long life. Those most involved in their jobs did best and lived much longer than more laid-back fellow workers.

A third project based at Rush Medical Center followed 1,238 elderly people living in the community and found those with a higher purpose in life had a mortality rate about half that of the others.

This research involved large numbers, was funded by major organizations such as the National Institute of Mental Health and reports were subject to peer review. But there are limits on what can be taken away from these studies. A major point is that correlation, the simple association of two items, does not mean causation. Although there were attempts to control for other variables that might be causing the correlation.

The classification was based for the most part on answers to three questions: "Some people wander aimlessly through life, but I am not one of them"; "I live life one day at a time and don't really think about the future"; "I sometimes feel as if I have done all there is to do in life." This kind of self-reporting is subjective and may change from day-to-day.

The takeaway point here is that research of this nature is indeed difficult to wade through, but well worth the effort. We just need to retain a certain amount of skepticism.

Now, back to the family that I started with. From my distance, I see it as having a strong sense of purpose in providing food, shelter, and love through the Great Depression and beyond. Nothing can be more satisfying.

I need to return here to the finding above that being "laid back" did not contribute to better health and lowered mortality. The data and my work as a therapist convince me that stress significantly and negatively impacts both outcomes.

Good luck to all of us in the continuing search for a sense of purpose, focus, and intent.

Journalism a Rapidly Changing Business

The demographics are not moving in a favorable way for the newspaper world. Three-fourths of the readers are over age 45 and the tilt increases dramatically with the higher age categories, leading to predictions that as my generation dies off, so will the newspaper. Publishers across the country, including the *Democrat's*, argue that talk about a death watch is not only premature but wrongheaded, as they point to changes being made to meet the competition. This may involve a little whistling in the dark, but they make some good points.

I have been a reader of the *Democrat* for 59 years and before that had a hand in the business. At age 13, along with others of about the same age, my peers and I had total responsibility for getting *The Newport News Daily Press* to subscribers. We picked up the papers, folded them so they could be thrown from a bike, and every Friday went house to house to collect. The paper did not charge me for the business lessons learned, including the fact that there are deadbeats that cheat 13-year-old kids. Now, having established my credentials, I offer a few observations on the current crisis.

Let me get a few negatives out of the way before moving on to other things. I confess to having complained about the *Democrat* for these 59 years, privately and sometimes publicly. Bashing the local paper is as American as apple pie, and I am as patriotic as the next person. Here are a few of the things that trouble me with the current paper. All those blown-up pictures, taking up entire pages, are certainly not worth a thousand words. And I know I am being a hypocrite when I say that all this unedited blogging is not necessarily a good thing. For the life of me, I cannot understand why anyone would read that State-by-State page that tells us how the corn crop is coming in Ohio. I understand the reasons for limited investigative reporting but wish it was otherwise. Besides all this, the paper does not publish all my op-eds.

But I am standing with the *Democrat*, rooting for it. (It does have several decent columnists.) Many mornings as I walk up the driveway about 4 a.m. the paper hits the gravel and is my companion as I start the day, sometimes for 15 minutes, usually a bit more. On June 8th I was shocked when I realized I had been reading with interest for over an hour. (OK, sometimes when reading I drop off for a 10 or 15-minute nap. Not that day.) There was great coverage of the search for a president for FSU. The word *bizarre* doesn't do justice to it, and if it was written up as fiction, an editor would reject it as overdrawn. The writers cast a helpful light on the players and the process, including developments such as the modification of an ad appearing in *The Chronicle of Higher Education* so that "loyalty to FSU" was a major qualification for candidacy as president.

There was similar coverage of what was, and was not, accomplished by the legislature, accompanied by little details such as the number of Republican leaders who believe that global warming is a hoax.

Then there is all the rest that we take away from the *Democrat*. It tells us more about Tallahassee than any other source. The calendar of coming events reminds us of the hundreds of interesting things going on. There are stories of people in need and how we can help. People doing good get some recognition. We get a fair exposure to major local issues surrounding health care, law enforcement, public budgets, etc.

Best wishes to the *Democrat* as it deals with the challenges it faces, not the least of which is keeping a wall of some sort between business needs and independent journalism.

Observations from Old Folks at a Wedding

My father lived with us for 16 years before dying at age 98. After being out somewhere he would return to say, "I was the oldest person in the room," a status he did not seek. I thought of him last week when we were sitting with about 200 people at a family wedding party in Raleigh, and I whispered to Betty, "We are the oldest people in the room." Full circle.

Ten of us were at table number 11, with Betty's siblings and their mates, thoughtfully located in the back of the room close to the bathrooms. Knowing that in a few weeks we would be flying to Davis, California, for the wedding of a grandson, and with the loudness of the music killing any possibility of conversation, I reflected on changes that have occurred since 1950, the year we were married. Changes small and not so small. Here is a sample, accompanied by a few words of advice.

The younger guests already have a hearing loss from exposure to music at the level we were experiencing and there is not much help for them. But the oldsters should be given quality earplugs upon entry to the room. In 1950, many wedding ceremonies contained the word "obey" and the phrase, "If anyone has any reason why this couple should not be joined in matrimony..." How quaint.

No matter how carefully you rehearse and plan for the wedding, only about a third of the spoken words will be heard. Knowing this ahead of time will help with not getting too upset by this failure.

After the hundreds of weddings that I must have attended, I can offer this advice: Don't ask the best man to speak. I have no explanation for it, but they tend to go on and on about happenings that are meaningful to only a very small circle. (This observation does not apply to the wedding we just attended.)

At one point in the evening, I noticed that a friend seated across the room looked as if he might be hearing something. When asked if there was anything he could pass on to us, he provided the following: love, laughter and the Lord make for a good marriage; traditions are important; the word "faith" was a key part of the ceremony; the building of strong families doesn't happen without good values and hard work. In all of this, there was no generation gap.

Dancing can be great fun, as it was at this wedding. Everybody was on the floor. The best I can tell is that the only requirements were to stay on your feet, shake your hips, pump your arms overhead. No need for a partner in all this, in contrast to our 1950 slow waltzes and close dancing. An astonishing 80 or 90 percent of the dancers could sing along with four hours of music. Of course, we didn't know a single line of the lyrics.

As the evening wound down and the bride and groom moved among the tables saying goodnight, I thought about what I would say if they had solicited some advice. My thoughts were guided in part by a book Betty gave me for Father's Day, *How About Never — Is Never*

Good For You? by Bob Mankoff, cartoon editor of the New Yorker. I would have encouraged them to lighten up, have some fun, work to keep humor significant in their life. It wouldn't hurt to look together at cartoons focused on marriage (thousands of such cartoons are readily accessed online).

Learn to Navigate the 'Helpers'

Yesterday I was on an elevator with one other person who looked like he was about age 11, but probably was about mid-30s.

He said to me, "Do you mind if I tie your shoelace?" I quickly dropped the papers I was carrying, tied the shoelace and thanked him. He said, "Oh, I didn't know you could bend over like that." I stepped into a multi-level parking garage and paused for a second, holding my keys while trying to remember where I left the car. A voice behind me, that of a security guard, said, "Give me your keys." He took them, pushed several buttons I didn't know existed, and there in the distance, my car horn started blowing along with flashing lights.

I was parked in a garage (yes, I do a lot of that) and was backing up very carefully, using both the side and rear mirrors, when I heard a scrunch. A truck, parked at a right angle to me, had a very long trailer hitch stuck under my bumper.

By the time I got out of the car, three men were standing there while an 88-pound woman was bouncing up and down on the bumper. She succeeded in freeing my car, and all four assured me that it could have happened to them.

I was talking to my sister-in-law about my older brother, Bill, who probably has more problems than I. He is allowed to walk several blocks in his neighborhood and had just returned to say that he couldn't go out anymore. Two cars driven by women, total strangers, had stopped to ask him if he needed help.

Now, all of this happened to me in a very short period of time. I am not creative enough to make it up. There was a lesson in there for me.

I'm turning pro — giving up my amateur status as an old man. In a previous column, I reviewed the evidence supporting the idea that forgiving another person does great things for the forgiver. Something like that may be operating here.

In all four instances above, the helpers had to feel good about themselves. (I have some guilt about not letting the man tie my shoelace, and certainly will the next time.) It may be that I made them think about their grandfathers. And maybe they don't have grandparents. Or may have neglected them. Whatever.

If you're a peer of mine, you might want to consider joining with me. I plan to move about deliberately with one shoelace untied, actually and metaphorically. There is some pleasure in knowing that I am in control while increasing others' self-esteem.

There is one problem. Turning pro implies that money is involved in some way and I have not come up with a means of collecting for these services.

If you can help, I am easily spotted in a parking garage, driving a 1997 white Mercury Grand Marquis with less than 80,000 miles.

Sunday, July 13, 2014

People Can Make a Difference with Their Actions

The front page of the July 1 *Tallahassee Democrat* was devoted to Jerome Gaines, our first black fire chief.

Now drop back 59 years for another *Democrat* front page story about two female Florida A&M students who were arrested after taking bus seats reserved for whites. This led to a successful bus boycott and the revocation of the ordinance requiring segregated seating.

In the negotiations, the city caved in except for the prohibition of people of different races sharing a seat. If Chief Gaines had been on the scene at that time, and the only open seat was next to a white person, he would be required to stand.

The whole scene was from the Theater of the Absurd.

It is not my intention here to revisit this complicated and dark story, except to note that our elected leaders and at least one judge came out of it with something worse than mud on their faces. My focus is on something more positive, which is that any crisis such as this one, tends to bring out people willing to put everything on the line in the pursuit of justice. (Note: senior writer Gerald Ensley said the *Democrat* reporters did a good job of reporting the story. Patronizing comments from the editor were another story.)

Here is a concrete example of putting things on the line, which I observed firsthand. Davis Thomas was the minister at the First Presbyterian Church from 1955 to 1968 (and later on a close friend of mine). When there was talk within the church about how to respond if blacks came to the church on a Sunday morning, he helped by saying that if they were not welcomed, the church could start looking for another minister the next day.

Under his leadership, the church set up a kindergarten which was integrated and provided scholarships for a number of children. He visited "freedom riders" who were in jail because of protests against segregation.

During the efforts to desegregate lunch counters, his was a familiar voice to city officials and law officers. By his actions and words from the pulpit, he showed us what we should be about. All of this he did quietly, no press conferences, no ranting and raving. It was not about him. (He probably would object to my mention of him here.)

There were costs to him — a certain amount of stress, members leaving the church. Possibly some in the black community feeling that the churches should have taken an even stronger stand.

Not many of us can muster the commitment Davis Thomas displayed. But today, anywhere you look around Tallahassee, you will see people in their 70s and 80s working in various ways to enhance social justice and fairness for the powerless.

Those of us who have been fortunate enough to retire with the confidence that we have enough to carry us through to the end should be thinking about the ways we use our time. Like it or not, we are in this thing together.

Go read Simon Van Booy's *The Illusion of Separateness*. Cry. Get out of the house. (Note: None of this is incompatible with my frequent advice to lighten up and have some fun.)

Sunday, July 27, 2014

Maintaining a Healthy Weight, and Why It Matters

Your eyes may glaze over when you see the words "obesity crisis." But try to keep them focused here as I outline a few basics.

- Indeed, the numbers confirm the existence of an obesity crisis, the severity of which has been underplayed.

- There is a backlash, calls to get off the backs of the overweight and denial rules the day.

- Life is particularly hard for the overweight elderly, but there are choices to be made.

- You are not allowed to compare yourself with the 900-pound Lansing, Mich., man who was forklifted out of a hole cut in the side of his house. But if you are overweight, you really should think seriously about what it means for you.

Some research suggests that modestly overweight elderly have lower death rates than individuals of healthy weights, and that being overweight may not increase the chances of developing certain cancers. This has prompted some to ask if being fat could be the new fit. (One doctor claimed that advising an elderly person to lose weight might result in charges of malpractice.)

Body size that is considered "normal" has escalated, with half of obese Americans believing that their weight falls in the "socially acceptable" range. There is less pressure to lose weight, more plus size models in the clothing ads and hospitals are buying bigger beds.

And yes, genes influence weight and it is obviously hard for some folks to lose pounds and keep them off. And yes, we do need to work on discrimination in work, love and play.

But look at this sample of benefits of maintaining a healthy weight: remaining independent, less damage to knees and hip joints, greater chance of getting a surgeon willing to do joint replacement, fewer aches and pains, lower risk for arthritis, increased self-esteem, improvement of things in the bedroom, fewer functional limitations. The ability to carry out the basics of daily life (getting out of a chair or bed, dressing yourself, etc.) has everything to do with the probability of not ending up in a wheelchair and nursing ward.

If you want to find some motivation, check out any continuing care facility and walk through the nursing floor. One other thing: a recent review of 20 long-term studies showed that obesity can shorten life expectancy by six to 14 years.

No one claims that maintaining a healthy weight at an advanced age is easy. But it can be done. Motivation is still the key. Try on this hypothetical situation: assume that an evil dictator has the power to make this rule: "Lose X pounds within X days or I will start killing your family one by one."

The TV program "The Biggest Loser" offers a $250,000 prize and the contestants shed hundreds of pounds. Companies concerned about medical and absenteeism costs related to obesity pay employees to trim down, and they do. Actor Steve Zahn lost 40 pounds for a movie role. And Christian Bale lost one-third of his body weight (63 pounds) for the movie "The Machinist" and for another role he regained more than he had lost. The point is that it can be done. (Particularly if we could all be given the right movie roles.)

So even if we do have a fat gene, doesn't the distinction of being human imply the occasional ability to overcome genetic wiring? Look at Mike Huckabee, the presidential candidate who lost 110 pounds and now runs marathons: "We tend to demonize industries, but it's my fault I was overweight. No one ever forced me to go to a McDonald's and order a triple cheeseburger or the largest fries they had, along with a milkshake."

He found a little motivation in 2003, with the onset of diabetes and a doctor's prediction that unless he lost weight he would be dead in a decade. Going on to write a book on weight loss, he made the subject a focus of his governorship.

In closing, I note that just-released research from Stanford Medical School suggests that overeating may not be the cause of America's obesity epidemic. The real culprit may be the lack of physical activity, a trend the researchers expected, but not of the magnitude they found.

So happy eating — just less. And happy activity – just more.

The State of Marriage

This is my final take on the state of marriage. Having been to three weddings within the last two months, spread across the country, I can assure you that it remains in high favor. We can argue about the definition of marriage, note that it is not a necessary requirement for living together, or having a child. We may express concern about the divorce rate of 50%, serial coupling, and infidelity (not sure about how to gauge the numbers for the latter). But the basics have not changed much, with our grandchildren looking for the same things we hoped for 64 years ago.

We wanted someone to love and love us. Someone willing to make the necessary accommodations as two people strive to become a functioning family unit. We wanted commitment and real intimacy, sexual and otherwise. We may not have thought in just these terms, but it was all there. Some of us were much more fortunate than others. (My nickname through college was *Lucky Pinky*.) The weddings we attended were happy affairs, the bride and groom surrounded by family and friends from across the country. Lots of laughter and tears. (There is something to the old axiom that we joke about death and cry over marriages.)

I might not be writing this column if our grandson had not asked his grandmother to write a poem to be read at his wedding. I think that it says in a compressed way some important things about love and endurance, and I would like to share it with you.

SONG OF SONGS

If we are telling of love, how does it begin?
A heady, giddy excitement, and then...
"Oh that you would kiss me with the kisses of your mouth
For your love is better than wine"...and suddenly, we two
Are drunk, intoxicated, and I am crazy for you.

So listen, come Love, I believe in you.
If life is a journey, come with me.
I'm in it for the long road, the U-Haul,
the heavy lifting. If I love in high emotion,
I know there is more, seeing every day
those who weep, who stumble and fall.
It is not who runs the fastest, but who runs the longest,
Who can handle the rough ground, for sometimes
We are not the smartest, the luckiest or strongest.
So listen to me, Love, I believe in us.

Let us stand up in front of people in joy
And celebration. Make a declaration,
Shout our intention to renounce aloneness
Make a commitment to each other and to love
Whose power, I think can transform us.

Transformed by love, (in spite of platitudes)
I know we are marrying not only the future
But also the past. Our errors, our childhood insecurities
Come tagging along. Our families, those who
Loved us before we loved each other, are on the side lines.
Even so, I'm stepping out in faith, singing my song
And until it turns into long silence, I want the words
To be tuneful, full of thanksgiving and forgiving.
May they be tender and honest, heart language from Solomon
"This is my beloved, and this is my friend."

This last trip to California reminds us that travel becomes increasingly hard. On the day we returned we were up at 6:30 and back home 16 hours later. If you young ones are planning to get married and would like to have us there, do it soon.

Sunday, August 17, 2014

Profanity Is on the Rise in Today's Society

In a recent email, a reader said that he was troubled by the wide acceptance of profanity, obscenity, and vulgarity. He went on to say, "In my opinion, it is better to have an eloquent command of language so that any thought can be expressed with color and vibrancy."

Shortly after receiving this message. I came across the following posting: "You hear it on TV, in the movies, music, at the office, in the stores, on schoolyards, in churches, etc. What has happened to our society that curse words are so acceptable these days?"

It is a subject that had not particularly caught my attention except for an observation that familiarity had deprived certain words and phrases of any shock value. (Something akin to the inflation that has enveloped the exclamation mark. A singular exclamation mark is not to be seen and soon it will take !!!!! to have any effect.)

I hasten to add that there was a period in my youth when I spent more time in a pool room than I should have, and held short-term jobs in a shipyard and repossessing used cars with a small loan company. All of this exposing me to considerable cursing and the gift of immunity.

My reader's letter raised a question about generational differences on the subject and I went online to see what could be learned. By happenstance, I hit on the work of Timothy Jay, psychologist at Massachusetts College of Liberal Arts, who has studied swearing for more than 30 years. Here is a sample of his findings:

- There are over 70 different common taboo swear words in English, but 10 words account for 80 percent of the usage. (You could probably name about seven of them.)

- Swearing accounts for about 0.5 percent of daily speech.

- The headline of one of his articles read, "Children are Swearing More Often, at Earlier Age." Swearing takes off between ages 3 and 4 and becomes adultlike by 11 or 12. Young adults report that they learned swear words from parents, peers, and siblings, not the mass media.

- The Fox broadcast network showed the greatest per-hour increase in use of profanity from 2005 to 2010, with an increase of 269 percent.

- We swear in reaction to something painful or unpleasant but it also reduces pain. Cursing is said to double the time that a hand can be held in freezing water.

- In over 10,000 episodes of public swearing by children and adults, rarely did the researchers see negative consequences. Many public taboo words can produce positive effects (e.g., humor, camaraderie, stress management, a substitute for physical aggression and facilitation of joking or storytelling).

Other investigators agree with Jay's conclusion that there has been a significant increase in swearing, but point out that younger generations are more concerned about the increase in racist, sexist and homophobic remarks. The rise in TV profanity has resulted in the availability of devices that mute foul language and skip objectionable scenes in movies.

I should note here that most of the literature is focused on public cursing, with little to say about that which occurs privately. You don't have to worry about what may come from your lips when the head comes in contact with an open cabinet door or you drop and break a favorite bowl.

Now, back to my readers mentioned at the top of this column. I am with them in acknowledging the power of words and a rich vocabulary as the default setting. Having said that, we can accept that there are times when the right swear word can add a desirable punch and intensity to the conversation.

Growing Older Is Like Having a Second Childhood

Two-year-old Olivia, one of our great-grandchildren, was in town last week.

Wait! Wait! Don't touch that dial! I am not going to bend your ear with boring tales of how marvelous she is, as easy as that would be. No, I am going to write primarily about me, using her as a kind of anchor. My second childhood is matching with her first.

She has only two states of being: sleeping or moving. She's almost never still, even when she is being read to — so much so that some observers might conclude that she has a movement disorder. So do I. Ever since James Parkinson befriended me about five years ago.

Olivia is pretty good with a fork and so am I. But it would be an unusual meal if some food could not be found in our laps and under the table.

She is only two so you will not be surprised to learn that she likes being the center of attention (especially since she recently acquired a brother). I no longer have much need for that.

Both of us drop things.

With her constant motion she bumps into things and her parents keep Band-Aids close by. It is a rare day when I am Band-Aid free, and I'm never entirely free of bruises.

I would guess that she cries a little less than most 2-year-olds. I don't know what the crying norm is for an octogenarian, but I find that I produce tears of happiness or sadness more frequently these days.

She can put on a long skirt and move across a room twirling madly. I don't have a skirt and would be on the floor before completing the first twirl.

Olivia never has a day without laughter and joy. Me too.

I do not tell jokes about aging and toileting and guess that Olivia is with me in that.

She is the only child I have known that goes off to bed happily and without fuss. Told that it is bedtime, she blows everyone a kiss and gets in bed. I am a lot like that but she gets about 10 hours of sleep compared with my five.

I am better than she is with buttons and tying shoelaces, but not much. Both of us need a little help at times.

Olivia will never wear a tie and I will probably get by with just a few more times.

I have some hearing loss and have noted that there are times when she seems unable to hear her parents.

My posture is stooped. Olivia is as straight as a bedpost.

Now you have to admit that given an 84-year gap, we have a surprising amount in common, not the least of which is greeting each new day with a sense of wonder and pleasure. She may not yet feel gratitude, but I do.

Some People Are Gone but Are Not Easily Forgotten

Periodically I like to call attention to an individual who has made a difference but has not much been in the public eye. This is by way of reminding ourselves that in this time of despair when the bad guys seem to be in total control, it is still possible to beat City Hall.

Gerontologist Bill Bell would be blowing out 100 candles on Sunday, had he not slipped away some years ago. Longtime Tallahasseeans might recall him as the husband of Budd Bell, a more visible activist. In her work, she tended to take the oxygen out of the room while Bill came along in his deliberate style replacing it.

As a professor in the Department of Urban and Regional Planning at Florida State University, he did the groundwork for what is now a significant program in gerontology. Step by step he obtained start-up federal funding and brought together faculty from across the university, all focused on teaching and research on the problems of aging.

A good part of his life was spent in organizing workshops, writing position papers, lobbying legislatures and building networks at the local, national and international level. A less committed person would not have made it through all those tedious meetings.

His interests were broad, but always related to the rights and needs of the disadvantaged, rural poor, and more fragile slice of the community — reducing the number of older people in mental hospitals, providing public guardianships and transportation for the elderly. Jo Ann Hutchinson, former executive director of the Commission for the Transportation Disadvantaged, credits him with making possible millions of annual trips to doctors, work, senior centers and other activities of daily living.

In the course of working together on a book we co-authored, as well as other related projects, I got to know the man's professional life well. Through contact with Budd and his daughter Bonnie, I learned some more personal details that defined his character.

He was a hands-on helper. Loved sports. Tutored a football player to help him keep his academic status. Mentored a Korean doctoral student and helped him and his family find housing and get acclimatized. Loaned a young single mother money to hire a lawyer and sent her home with some of Budd's dinner cooking, following up by mowing her grass and taking her kid to a football game.

He would never mention any of this.

Bill gave away countless containers of food (and wanted the containers back). He maintained an absolutely spotless oven in which many delicious things were cooked since he and Budd entertained a wide range of people.

In closing, here is a quote that I saw just today. "They say such nice things about people at their funerals that it makes me sad to realize that I am going to miss mine by just a few days." (Garrison Keillor, *Good Poems for Hard Times.*)

Bill would be embarrassed, but I wish he could hear how much he is still appreciated.

Have We Lost the Ability to Be Rational?

I have always been a believer in the value of education in facilitating rationality — that is, the ability to discern what is probably the truth in a given argument.

With the end of the war in 1945, there was a surge in education as a result of the G.I. Bill (and I was a beneficiary). Seventy years later education is at a peak, but rationality not so much so. Note the following.

Half of the population believe that the earth is less than 10,000 years old. A third believe in UFOs, that the FDA suppressed a cure for cancer, that vaccines cause autism and Obama was born in Kenya (never mind the Hawaiian birth certificate). A quarter think that astrology is real, not just for entertainment. Twelve percent of Americans believe that the CIA deliberately infected African-Americans with HIV under the guise of hepatitis inoculation (Russian propaganda).

And just this week, a candidate for the presidency of a large university declined to respond to a question about global warming and evolution. This could have been a political decision.

If you have nothing better to do, Google "stupid beliefs" and stand back from the deluge. Within minutes, you can find thousands of people with the same weird belief.

The absence of rationality can be found in all areas of life and it seems that increased education has not had much impact on our belief systems. We believe what we want to, search for evidence to support what we think we know, dismiss anything that doesn't confirm, and double down when challenged.

So, what to do? Turn to science, which requires adherence to empirical study, independent verification and replication. But by definition, it is subject to error, and what is taken as gospel at one time is later seen as folly.

On any one issue, you can always find an expert who takes the opposite side. I don't want to shock anyone here, but scientists share our common humanity and have been known to use selective evidence for a variety of purposes. But not all of us can learn quantum mechanics and thus we have to trust them, with all the messiness.

We tell ourselves lies, not unlike the citizens of Lake Wobegon, "where the women are strong, the men are good-looking, and all the children are above average." Skepticism should always be a traveling companion.

Now, back to the concern I expressed above about the failure of education to rein in faulty thinking. If nothing else, we need to train scientists and emphasize critical thinking.

But with the current emphasis on STEM, we also have to be sure to educate a significant number of philosophers, humanists, anthropologists and the like, and have them looking over the shoulders of the scientists.

Sunday, September 28, 2014

We Have a Complex Relationship with Our Phones

It is early Saturday morning and Betty and I are sitting in a cubicle of the emergency room, waiting for the doc to come back and tell us what he thinks about Betty's ugly swollen wrist. We look up to see daughter Ann standing in the doorway, with a concerned look and a, "What's up?"

We tell her the little we know and she asks, "Where is your cell phone?" We are not sure, maybe in Betty's purse. She reminds us that not only should we have the phone with us, but that it doesn't work unless it is on. She then explains that not finding us at home and knowing that we had been to Urgent Care the night before, she had been calling every ER in Tallahassee.

This exchange prompted me to think a little about our relationship with phones, having heard other boomers complain about their parents' reluctance to get aboard.

We have seven phones: three mobile phones given to us by the children some years ago, a phone on Betty's desk that is used for certain long distance calls, a neat little flat phone on Betty's bedside, an old flip-top cell that has been dropped so many times that you cannot determine the brand and a cell that is just short of being a smartphone.

We are not total Luddites when it comes to electronic devices, having computers for years and early owners of Kindles. But our phones are troublesome and seem to have radically different personalities. Some like to be tapped, some like for you to drag your finger across their faces — not always in the same direction.

Some require a certain number before you can call out; for reasons we don't understand, some require the entering of a secret (to us) code. I would guess that in trying to answer an incoming call, we manage to break the connection about 50 percent of the time.

At this point, you might be wondering why we don't come into 2014, kill the landline and all the phones except Betty's cell, and purchase another cell for Kent.

For one thing, Betty and I have different styles. She gets attached to things, wastes nothing, holds on to things until she finds somebody in need. I keep an empty inbox and readily move things out the door. But when it comes to phones, we have a lot in common.

At 87, we don't want to squander the limited time remaining to really learn our way with the phones. We are not likely to break a hip racing to get a recorded phone call that begins with "Hello seniors...".

Calls are more and more like the mail, with only about 10 percent of any interest. We don't want 24/7 connectivity with access to the world in our pockets. We will never be in camp with that 58 percent of smartphone owners who check their mail every hour, or the 30 percent who check their phones while dining with others, or the 54 percent who check their phones in bed (Survey by Harris Interactive,

2012). And we don't have to worry about the World Health Organization declaration that mobile phones contribute to a higher risk for reduced sperm and tumors.

Our aim is to get far below the U.S. household average of 5.7 devices connected to the internet.

There is something to be said for the time we grew up in when a long distance call meant somebody had died.

So if you have trouble getting through to us, it is not personal. Do the old thing of dropping by to see us. But in the interest of full disclosure, we have in the front door one of those little holes that lets us see who is ringing the bell.

The Cost Analysis of Living Past 75

The September issue of *The Atlantic* contains an article by Ezekiel Emanuel, bioethicist and advisor on health care policy. Under the provocative title, "Why I Hope to Die at 75", he lays out his reasoning and set off considerable chatter on the internet.

Emanuel has written at length but his main point is that people living beyond 75 eat up health resources and are remembered as "feeble, ineffectual, even pathetic." Our desperation to extend life is "misguided and potentially destructive." He spells out in detail what he plans to do and not do, and his wish is that we come along with him.

His article renewed concerns about "death panels" and rationing of health care. Critics responded with long lists of older people who made their major contributions after age 75. Some readers who knew that Emanuel had a lot to do with the Affordable Care Act, complained about his setting up what they consider to be a failure. Others who knew of his opposition to a single payer health plan fault him for taking that position, since it is the only viable plan.

Regrettably, we will not be around to see what Mr. Emanuel does when he turns 75. We can hope that a single-payer health plan will have kept him healthy and he can take advantage of the little wiggle room built into his article.

If for nothing else, we should be grateful to him for stimulating a conversation on some important issues.

I will never meet Mr. Emanuel, and that will probably not be a loss for either of us. Reading between the lines, I think his definition of "making a contribution" would relate to major scientific advancements or outstanding works of art or history, usually involving peer approval and recognition. My definition would include the sanctity of all human life, not just the elderly. Anything short of this would require arbitrary decisions that we are not ready to make.

For some, this can be a heavy burden, and with a rapidly expanding number of old people, we may have to expand the services currently being provided through voluntary and government programs. (Note that many of these services are staffed by people past age 75.)

Mr. Emanuel's argument is highly personal and so is the following. I am on the verge of 87, have some cognitive impairment (Parkinson's) and know the natural history and direction of most neural disorders. I plead guilty to sucking up more than my share of medical care, moving around the country for the best I could find. My movement from giver to taker occurred some time ago and I harbor no illusions on where I would fall on any cost/benefit analysis.

My family knows well at what point I would like to have the plug pulled. But not yet. At lunch today I had two Fat Boy ice cream sandwiches (minis), a Nutty Buddy after dinner and our California daughter comes in tonight for a week stay. It can't get much better than that.

There's Nothing Like Old Friends

For 40 or so years we have come together annually with six other couples for a long weekend. We recently had lunch with seven of the group in the North Carolina mountains, and for some time now the goodbye hugs come with awareness that this might be our last such hug. Of our original 14, we have already lost three, and two no longer travel.

This lunch caused me to reflect on what it means to have such long-term friends. We have come to know each other through the sharing of our individual successes and failures, the facing of health problems, concerns about children and grandchildren. Of course, there is mutual affection and the sharing of values and interests. (This particular group formed through church associations.) But there is also history, the sheer length of time. And I am reminded of the old musical round, "Make new friends but keep the old. One is silver but the other is gold."

I think key ingredients in lasting relationships are forgiveness, tolerance of errors and mistakes, a willingness to hang tight, talk, try and try again.

The Valentine's Group (left to right): Janie Enniss, Pat Kennedy, Wally Kennedy, Carlisle Harvard, Buddy Enniss, Dottie Thornburg, Bud Hendry, Sally Telford, George Telford, Betty Miller, Joe Harvard, Kent Miller, Lacy Thornburg, & Pat Hendry (not pictured)

Then there are new friendships, the pleasure of meeting someone with whom you feel an immediate connection, an openness that can be most exciting.

Muhammad Ali tells us that, "Friendship is the hardest thing in the world to explain. It is not something that you learn in school. But if you haven't learned the meaning of friendship, you really haven't learned anything."

Here are some markers that will tell you when you have a friend: when in an emergency you can call them at 4 a.m.; when you are comfortable in silence; when one person says to another, "What. You too? I thought that I was the only one." (C.S. Lewis); when a person knows all about you and still loves you; when you forget what you have forgiven but remember what you have received.

By any standard, we are close friends, and the visit led to a conversation with wife Betty about whom and how many close friends we had. It was an interesting exercise and prompted me to take a look at what was being said about friendship, to look for numbers and conclusions that were based on surveys, social science and the reasoning of experts. Here are a few things that floated to the top for me.

- Even in a perfect marriage, there is a need for intimacy that goes beyond one person. This is particularly true for older people following the death of a spouse, and new friends can be found well into old age.

- We tend to make friends with people much like ourselves in backgrounds, interests, etc. (Shocking, isn't it?)

- The average number of close friends for Americans is two.

- In the western world, Germans have the fewest friends, but put a premium on loyalty.

- Cows are more stressed when alone and are good at making friends.

- I think that I already knew that dogs love other dogs and cats don't want another cat on the block. (I know, not true of yours.)

- The amount of time devoted to our computers and smartphones works against friendship.

Now, back to the friends I mentioned at the top. We are following the natural history of aging and will not be seeing one another as often. Which means that to keep contact we will have to fall back on Skype, phones and even an old-fashioned handwritten note. Digital technology is making it easy to stay in touch.

Go see a friend. If there are fences to mend, get going.

Sunday, October 26, 2014

How Do We Really Make Decisions?

We have two cars — a 17-year-old Mercury with 80,000 miles (my gym car because I sweat a lot), and a 2005 Subaru with 52,000 miles. Last week as we exited the driveway, Betty asked if we want to buy one last new car.

Today's lesson is centered on how we make decisions.

I think of it in terms of cost and benefits. A new car is safer (backup camera), no trips to garage for a while, new car smell, etc. On the cost side is the time taken to shop, alternative ways of spending $30K, etc. We make the list, talk and come to a decision. Or decide not to decide. Yes? No. Not quite.

Economists and business school professors are joining the psychologists in searching for ways to improve decision-making to better reflect one's self-interests.

In my graduate school days of clinical training (early 1950s) there was some emphasis on the significance of early childhood experiences, family dynamics, catharsis and the impact of the unconscious. A little later the behaviorists followed with a greater emphasis on science and empirically based treatment.

Currently, it is the neurologists getting all the attention, urged on by advances in brain imaging. They believe that given a little time, they will have the brain well mapped and will have found the mutation that leads to a preference for dark chocolate over milk chocolate, and nearly everything else.

There is increasing evidence that our choices are driven by forces outside of our consciousness. We know that what sells in the school cafeteria can be manipulated by placement in the line, that the image associated with a given model car impacts sales, and a thousand other forces are at work to prevent us from making decisions in our own self-interest.

We are co-conspirators by seeking information that supports what we already believe and ignoring data that are not consistent with our beliefs. Conservatives are guided by FOX News and liberals get their guidance from the other end of the spectrum.

Another hindrance to good decision-making relates to the abundance of choices. We are overwhelmed by the number of TV channels, supermarkets have an average of 42,700 items, the number of different healthcare options is mind-boggling. Sometimes making a choice just involves too much energy and time to make it worthwhile.

So, given this outline of a problem, what's to be done? Recognizing the problem is the first step. Paying some attention to what is being said by the parties at the other end of the spectrum is not going to hurt (admittedly, it may hurt a little at first).

Work some at getting the facts surrounding given choices; maybe steal a little time from the opinion pages. Find a friend you respect and who will be honest in conversation with you. Get lucky.

Now, back to our question of buying a car. At the moment it is on hold. But I suspect that if either of us said, "Oh, what the hell, let's go get one," we would.

Relationship Between Age and Politics Not Clear-cut

"If you are not a liberal when you're 20, you have no heart. If you are not a conservative by the time you're 30, you have no brain."

This saying, or something like it, has already been attributed to a long list of famous people or I would take it as my own (assuming I could modify it a bit). It is a good jumping-off point for today's topic: age and politics.

Much of the survey research on this topic has compared four generations (I draw heavily from the respected Pew Research Center): Millennials, ages 18-33; Generation X, ages 34-49; Baby Boomers, ages 50-68; Silent Generation, ages 69-86. (At 87, I must be statistically dead.)

There is a widespread belief that with increasing age, the elderly tend to embrace conservative social positions. Explanations for this generally accepted relationship include the notion that a pull to the right comes with marriage, the first child, a mortgage and higher income. There are suggestions that young voters leaning left are pushed by genes, hard-wired to shift over time, before and after brain changes in the mid-20s. Psychologist Robert McCrae, at the National Institute of Aging, believes that as we age, changes in gene expression may alter openness, conscientiousness and other traits. In short, brain changes play a part at both ends of the age spectrum.

And to further muddy the water, there are researchers who argue that the premise that older people are so much more conservative is false, and they are able to muster sufficient data to gain publication in scientific journals.

The Republican Party has struggled for some time to appeal to the young. But there is real trouble ahead for them unless something unexpected happens. The millennials are considerably more liberal than other generations, there are a lot of them, and about 50 percent are Democrats, contrasted with 34 percent leaning to the GOP. (The 16 percent not accounted for were unaffiliated or third party.)

Some of the most dramatic differences within the Republicans center on social issues such as immigration, the environment, homosexuality, social safety nets and the role of government. About half of Republican millennials think that corporations make too much profit. (In a total aside, I was surprised by a finding by American National Election Studies in 2012, that the correlation between family income and party identification was 0.13, practically zero.)

The general profile of younger Democrats was much more in alignment than was the case with the Republicans.

Another problem for the Republicans lies in the nation becoming less religious. In every region of the country and every denomination, membership is down. The religiously unaffiliated, who tend to vote Democratic, are now a significant slice of the demographic pie. All of this has implications for the Republican Tea Party base of fundamentalist Southern whites.

From all of this, I come away with some confusion. Are we older people rigid, cantankerous, highly conservative? I know a large group of people who don't fit that definition.

Current research is interesting and gives us some useful generalizations which tend to lead to stereotypes. Beware. It takes some effort to judge others as the individuals they are.

Sunday, November 9, 2014

Aging, Cognitive Impairment, and Driving

Earlier this year we decided to go down to Gainesville to see if the people at Shands know anything new about Parkinson's. Our California and Pennsylvania daughters thought that was a good chance to visit our Tallahassee daughter and check on the parents (and possibly to check on the status of our will, and related stuff).

So as we moved around between the differing specialists, there were always six of us in the room (Betty, three daughters, Mr. Parkinson's, me). I mention this because when you put four strong-willed people together in a room you don't have to be a psychologist to know that they have some impact on group dynamics and what comes through may be contaminated. I suspect that most of the docs forgot all about me in two days, but I would bet they remember that guy that brought four women with him.

I hasten to say that my experience was most positive and I was given a thorough workup. A lot of letters involved: MRI, CT, EKG, EEG, EMG. A lot of viewing, reviewing, talking, walking, poking, twisting of arms and legs. I felt that I had been in a 150-pound wrestling match, mismatched with someone from a higher class. But I did learn some things from all the reports given to me.

One of the positive findings was that I had a symmetrical smile. Not as positive were the signs of aging. (Really.) But most troubling was the diagnosis of Mild Cognitive Impairment (MCI). I have a feeling this is the diagnosis of the year and you might as well learn enough to be part of the discussion.

Studies show that about 12 percent of people with MCI progress to Alzheimer's in one year, while others with MCI decline slowly over a few years and then pick up a diagnosis of progressive dementia. Researchers tell us that this happens in about three years, to somewhere between 40 to 65 percent with a diagnosis.

For a diagnosis of MCI, the brain cell changes occur in one area of the brain that is responsible for a specific function. But over time the decline can spread to other areas affecting language and the use of the hands in delicate activities.

My layman take on all of this is that there are not many crisp boundaries between areas. My scientific background leads to a certain amount of skepticism about the validity of some of the numbers and conclusions that I quote. They may be the best we have at the moment, but don't hold them tightly.

All of this, in the context of Parkinson's, induces changes in gait, balance, posture, speech, swallowing, sleep, drooling, tremors and a lot more. In a rather non-scientific analogy, the death of brain cells leaves one with areas that look like Swiss cheese. The good news is that most of us don't have all those problems and life moves on in satisfying ways.

Meanwhile, I close with an example of this crazy world.

I am sure that everyone reading this thinks that they are good drivers, just as I do myself. But I thought that a little objectivity might be helpful and decided to get an on-the-road evaluation.

A quick call to the Department of Highway Safety and I was off to where they told me to go. I explained to the receptionist what I wanted and she asked to see my papers. What papers?

She continued to ask for the non-existent papers and I persisted in telling her I just wanted a test and I would be happy to pay for it. Can't be done, she says. Have to have a doctor's orders.

She had never seen anyone voluntarily ask for a test and reminded me that they could take my license if I failed. Yep. That was the point.

So at the moment, I still think I am a good driver.

Sunday, November 16, 2014

Physical Exercise and the Brain

I know. You are tired of being told to lose some weight and exercise. You would like to just live the life of the mind. And you might fit in with that group of people who give a higher priority to staying "mentally sharp" than to social security and physical health.

For a while now you have been hearing footsteps behind you and an awareness of some memory problems. Along with many of your friends, you may have started exercising your brain by working on crossword puzzles, forcing yourself to learn something new, memorizing poetry, etc. These exercises certainly don't do any harm, and may even do some good. I am not up on the research on this topic, but from what I have seen there is reason to withhold judgment.

But there is a rapidly growing body of research about another form of exercise that has a favorable impact on the brain: physical. Good old-fashioned aerobic running, brisk walking, swimming, cycling, jogging. These activities are said to protect an aging brain far better than mental or leisure exercises.

The following sample of tidbits and quotes will give you a sense of what we are learning.

- The number one cognitive complaint of older adults is the decrease in mental efficiency and memory decline. Research from the Brain Health Center at the University of Texas focused on subjects aged 57-75 and found that exercisers had an increase in brain blood flow. "Physical exercise may be one of the most beneficial and cost-effective therapies widely available to everyone to elevate memory performance. These findings should motivate adults of all ages to start exercising aerobically."

- People who regularly participate in aerobic exercise have greater scores on neuropsychological function and performance tests compared to people that participate in strength and flexibility training. (Wikipedia. "Neurobiological Effects of Physical Exercise").

- Researchers from Canada and the Netherlands did a twenty-six-week study of women who were between 70 and 80 years old. The group that did aerobic exercise had significantly increased hippocampal volume at the end of 26 weeks. (*British Journal of Sports Medicine*).

- Seven hundred people living in the United Kingdom had brain scans when they were 73. Three years earlier the study participants were questioned about their leisure and physical activities. People in the study who were most physically active had larger brain volumes of gray and normal white matter and less brain atrophy. "Staying mentally sharp as you age may have more to do with working out than working on crossword puzzles, new research shows." (WebMD News Archive).

- Spatial memory is the part of memory responsible for regulating and encoding information about the surroundings and orientation in space and is primarily controlled by the hippocampus. Physically fit people show better performance on various spatial memory tasks. These findings have been confirmed in research with rats. (Wikipedia).

There is much more research like this, covering a number of positive effects of aerobic exercise: increased heart rate resulting in more oxygen to the brain; release of hormones that nourish the growth of brain cells; a drop in stress hormones; acts as a "first aid kit on damaged brain cells." (see brainhq.com).

We need to get with it. It helps to be told that exercising twenty minutes facilitates information processing and memory functions.

Family Reunions Show the Differences Between Generations

Family reunions get a bad rap. There is an entire industry devoted to one-liners and jokes about the subject, some of them crude, some clever. (I am not citing any here, but if you must look, you can do so by searching *jokes about family reunions*.) But the very fact that such an industry exists tells us that coming together is important. I think that many of us are motivated by an unconscious need to be in community, to love and be loved, to be accepted with warts and all. Family can sometimes provide that structure.

We just returned from a week-long reunion in Williamsburg, which included a reception celebrating the marriage of Betty's nephew, a Buddhist monk for the last 14 years. The bride was a Korean nun. While working together in England, they fell in love and took the plunge, knowing they would have to leave the Order.

For about a week they were surrounded by 40 some extended Davis family members, with an age spread from 17 to 87, who had traveled from coast to coast and points in between. Lots of fun, laughter, and noise. (Things may have moved along so well because with 40+

people in the room we could not hear one another and the result was a lot of smiling and nodding of heads.) Considerable nostalgia for the two of us, returning to sites at William and Mary, where we met 69 years earlier.

For the most part, we were a homogeneous group. Lots of highly educated people, lawyers, doctors, five or six college professors, librarians, and a long list of degrees beyond the undergraduate. (The G.I. bill was crucial in opening up higher education.) We had natives of Korea and Peru. At least five people had been divorced and remarried. Some of the younger couples among us were living together, postponing marriage.

Most of us are Democrats, but there were a few people who have not yet seen the light, and they were warmly accepted. Lots of discussions centered upon political issues. For most of us the church has been formative, but here again, we are spread out a bit on a continuum.

By the standards of the world, we are rich. Enough so that we could get off from work, travel distances, and gather in a nice setting. I suspect that every person in attendance had traveled abroad. Conversation touched on travel plans, the best cruises, and restaurants.

One of the surprises for me at the reunion was how well cousins had maintained contact with one another. The internet, Facebook, etc., making it easy for verbal and visual communication.

I give this short description of our family in order to contrast it with that of our parents (Kent's and Betty's).

Their financial status was impacted by the great depression. None of them traveled outside of the U.S. and only Betty's mother received some college education. (On the other hand, they lived close to one another as opposed to scattered across the country.)

For them, contact with family at any distance was difficult. A long distance phone call meant that there had been a death in the family or a crisis of some kind.

The divorce rate was markedly lower for our parents' generation (without arguing that it is a good or bad thing).

Life expectancy was considerably higher for those attending this reunion.

All in all, these are relatively dramatic differences.

We can't say much about whether the two groups differ in meeting the needs to "love and be loved". Some families are not strong enough to meet those needs and help has to be found elsewhere.

I think that the group assembled in Williamsburg had some awareness of this and wanted to strengthen the family ties. It will be interesting to see how our grandchildren characterize us 25 years from now.

Don't Let the Swindlers Get You

The odds are pretty good that some of you reading this column have been swindled.

An estimated $40 billion is skimmed annually in the United States, with one in five of us over age 55 admitting to having fallen for a hustle. A second survey found that one in five over age 65 had been financially abused in some way. These figures likely err on the low side because of shame at having been a fool, coupled with concern about losing independence.

The scammers are in high cotton, with a rapidly expanding population and easy means of stealing personal information. Some of the most common types are health care, counterfeit prescription drugs, funeral and cemetery charges, anti-aging products, sweepstakes, winning the lottery, and one of my favorites: a call from a California grandson, who lost his wallet, can't get in touch with his parents, and needs to have money wired to him. We recently received such a call, with the person identifying himself as Alex, the actual name of one of our grandsons. What hard-hearted grandparent can turn down that request? Apparently not many, because this particular hustle has been around for six years.

You might want to be looking over your shoulder since one researcher reports that more than 90 percent of financial abuse comes from family members and caregivers. (Not, of course, yours or ours.)

Fortunately, there is a lot of free help readily available. (Fraud Watch Network; ProtectSeniorsFromFraud.com; AARP's Fraud Fighter Call Center). The city of Tallahassee has a weekly course for seniors on how to avoid crime: eldercare.gov. There you will find checklists, etc., and suggestions for specific actions, some very simple, some more complex. e.g., sign up on the national do not call registry; get online access to bank/credit cards; give power of attorney to a younger family member; give up the landline phone for a cell phone (fewer calls are made to these); cut down the number of credit cards; reduce the volume of bulk mail by registering at the Direct Marketing Association's Mail Preference Service.

Of course, we have not done any of these things (do as I say not ...). But we have talked about it. The kids have never said a word and know little about our finances, beyond where to look for records. At the moment we consider ourselves at low risk for being scammed, knowing that status is tenuous, subject to change in an eye blink.

But if we hang on long enough, the time will likely come when we are vulnerable, incapable of managing our affairs. Our hope is that we will be open to advice from our children, turning things lose without feeling threatened or that we are losing our independence.

But not yet. And in the late 80s, who wants to devote much time to money matters?

Sunday, December 21, 2014

Sustaining Hope Not Easy, but Necessary

A recent news item referred to Pope Francis comforting a 10-year-old boy whose dog had died. He allegedly told him that someday we will see our animals again, that paradise is open to all God's creatures.

This prompted some to say we all should be vegans, others to quote the Bible: "The Lord sees even every sparrow that falls." (Subsequently, things were a little confused, with some saying the Pope was only speaking conversationally, others attributing the saying to Pope Paul VI, and a day later an admission that the media had screwed up badly. There was no 10-year-old boy, no dog.)

No matter. I have never spoken to the Pope, who is an interesting man, and no offense intended, I doubt if he knows much more than you and I do about our pets going to heaven. But there is no doubt that had there been such a boy and dead dog, the Pope would have comforted him, would have been inclusive and offered hope. We all live on hope, the desire and expectation of fulfillment. Without it, we are dead.

Current conditions suggest that sustaining hope may not be easy. Polls show that 80 percent of us do not trust the government, yet only a strong government can possibly address problems such as these: racism, climate change, Ebola, immigration, water purity, inequality, population expansion, science funding.

Meanwhile, in the last election, we turned over the running of the country to the small government people. Add to that, this article headline: "The Kochs eclipse the RNC (Republican National Committee)." The authors report that with their resources and reach, the brothers are more powerful than the RNC and get the blue ribbon for showing what money can do for you in politics. How much do you think they care about the problems mentioned above?

But take heart. That 80 percent distrust of government figure is misleading. Ask people about specific programs and they strongly endorse a significant number. There is a belief that by coming together we can improve the lives of many. At the moment there is a groundswell of energy and activism within the grassroots, a nation of believers in ideas that can institute change. If you are not already involved in some of this, you could give a little boost to keeping hope alive by doing so. Find a cause you believe in and join in.

December brings the singing of songs of peace and goodwill. A time to look forward, greet one another warmly, give presents, be nice to those with whom we disagree, come together with family, marvel at the promise of grand and great-grandchildren. A time for reflection, and possibly some break in routine. Fresh starts.

It all feels good. The danger comes as we move into winter, failing to keep our eyes and actions focused on some of the really tough challenges. Take as an example, the growth of the private prison industry, the massive incarceration of people of color. Being aware is a crucial first step, and retired people with time can help with this.

We have to be patient, knowing that change comes slowly, but it comes. The naysayers, the haters, those that turn to violence, are in a minority. In our lifetimes we have seen dramatic changes, but with a distance yet to travel. Hang in. Hope.

Sunday, January 4, 2015

Age and Appearance: Who Does Baby Look Like?

Over the holidays we had a large gathering of our extended family, including two great-grandchildren who are less than seven months old (never seen by some of the family). After a lot of oohing and aahing over the babies, the conversation turned to opinions about family resemblances. Some thought the child looked like the father; others could see features of the mother, an older sibling or other family member. Opinions were backed up by reference to the color of the eyes, the shape of the head, the length of the nose, etc. My interest was piqued because I had some affinity with those who believed that all babies looked alike (with an exception, of course, for my own daughters). Clearly, this was not the view held by my assembled family.

The conversation made me wonder if anyone had looked systematically at the dynamics of comparing a baby with relatives. Poking around a bit I found that indeed a number of people had written about the topic, without a consensus. Some reported that the child was said to look like the mother or the father on an even basis; some found for the father or mother. Research published in *Scientific*

Kent with great-grandson Kent Johnson, 2017

American concluded that people were better at matching photographs of a child with his or her father than the mother. It turns out that the father is the most likely choice, particularly if he is present during the conversation. (If not present, the figure drops by 27%.) A good reason for seeing a resemblance to the father is that it might encourage him to stay involved in the life of the child.

The picture is not so clear and your opinion may be as good as any. (If there were to be a rich uncle on the scene, I would be tempted to see a strong resemblance there.)

Now, let us move on to the proposition, *all old people look alike.* Most of the research has focused not on the general question but more on the notion that couples who stay together over time tend to look more alike. Sometimes the evidence is not all that visible but can be reliably detected by electronic devices. (One such device purports to assess 66 facial points.)

A number of explanations have been offered to explain this merging of expression. Possibly couples chose each other because they look similar at the outset. Also, after decades of shared emotions, and similar diets they may have similar fatty deposits and facial lines. Close couples may laugh a lot, utilizing the same facial muscles, and are empathetic, mimicking one another.

Of course, the natural history of aging – loss of hair, thinning of the face, wrinkles, etc., contributes to shared appearances.

There may be another simple explanation for our failure to see unique qualities of individuals, young or old. We tend to think of babies and the aged in the same manner we do whole classes of people that tend to be invisible to us: e.g., the homeless, other races, other social classes. It takes a conscious effort to see them.

Things to Do: Saving World, Conserving Energy

Things To Do. I noticed these words across the top of a notepad as I sat down with pen to outline a column. In some convoluted way, they made me think of Robert Love Miller, my father. At age 82, following the death of my mother, he came down from Virginia to live with us. He had no interest in sports, had no hobbies, and the best I can tell, may have been the only man in America of his generation who had never had a hammer in hand. In his eyes, without work he was nothing. He could not have put the words on it, but he needed Things To Do.

Living with us for 16 years (the last two in a nursing home with a pretty much empty head), he was the source of many family stories. This gentle man, with the limitations many of us display, found ways to survive with some satisfaction. As with most of us, he needed a place where he was respected, loved, counted on to appear for meals. But there were many lonely hours in between.

Suddenly our yard was raked as never before. He went across town to rake my sister-in-law's yard. He volunteered for Meals on Wheels.

Somehow he discovered and joined a group of retired men who drank coffee at McDonald's every morning, joined a Lutheran Church where he was often the oldest member. He found things to do that gave his life structure and satisfaction.

Now that I am several years older than he was when he came to us, I frequently have reflections of ways in which I have become more like him. One striking example occurred this morning. Betty called up from the downstairs bedroom, asking me to come down to water a plant. I did as asked, only to learn a few minutes later that I had replicated a frequent action of my father: watering an artificial plant. Finally, I had become my father!

I am sure that this and other similar actions on my part will lead to concerns about cognitive impairment. My only defense is the claim that I was highly focused on doing something about global warming and the Keystone XL Pipeline; in short, saving the world.

While I am playing defense here, let me say that I am not depressed. At my age, even the most mature and loving family is on watch for deterioration and apparently over the holidays some of the 12 to 15 family members thought that they caught a whiff of the black dog. I probably didn't talk as much as usual, but I did smile a lot. Couldn't get into the conversation in part because I couldn't hear some of the women on the other side of the room, and in part because I was apparently the only person in the room who didn't have an opinion about the plot and cast of all current movies and best sellers, which animals are on the endangered list, current foodie trends, etc. Alien country for me. I didn't think anyone wanted to talk with me about U.N. Resolution 1245 or the budget that will be coming out of Congress (well, maybe the latter).

Besides, if I am to help save the world I must conserve my energy. Lots of Things To Do, including pushing back against ageism. There is evidence to support the conclusion that negative stereotypes of the elderly are more common than those based on gender, race, and sexual orientation. As life expectancy continues to expand, so should the opportunity for the elderly to continue to contribute to society in meaningful and purposeful ways.

Sunday, January 18, 2015

A Laugh a Day Certainly Can't Hurt

OK Google. I am looking for something that does the following for old people: increases longevity; improves cognitive functioning; facilitates social binding; suppresses pain; mitigates depression; increases happiness; lowers blood pressure while increasing blood flow and oxygen intake.

Thanks. Got it: Laughter.

The study of laughter is a relatively new discipline, but the beginnings of a body of knowledge are in place. There is some evidence supporting all of the items above and there is hope that laughing will emerge as one of the most powerful medicines for chronic and degenerative conditions such as dementia, Alzheimer's, Parkinson's, and cancer.

Laughter and humor are not the same. Laughter is the physiological response to humor, involving gestures and a sound. Some 15 facial muscles stimulate the zygomatic major muscle (the lifting mechanism of the upper lip). A wave of electricity is said to sweep through the entire cerebral cortex, activating muscles throughout the body. Endorphins are released. Levels of the stress hormone cortisol drop after laughter, minimizing inflammation. T-cells are released. Who would have thought all of this, and more, could come out of a simple laugh.

Authorities believe that laughter is an unconscious response to social and linguistic clues, recognized by people in all cultures. We don't laugh much when alone (one study showing that we are 30 times more likely to laugh in the presence of another). It is difficult to laugh on demand and attempts to do so result in a "forced" sound.

There are significant gender differences, with women laughing more than men, who are more likely to be instigators (as is the boss, male or female). An analysis of personal ads across a number of sites revealed that women more often mentioned the desirability of a sense of humor. One researcher reports that the best indicator of the health of a relationship is the degree of laughter of the woman.

A lot of attention has been focused on the elderly. My inbox is flooded with jokes about wrinkles, memory and hearing loss, aging sex, night time peeing, keeping the medications straight, death, ageism. At least they are trying to keep us laughing.

In the face of all of these issues, the people we know are not much into denial, but taking things head on.

So, how valid is the impact of laughter implied in my opening comments? Yes, there is some evidence for all of it, but reason to be skeptical. Some of the research has passed the muster of publication in scientific journals. Research efforts have ranged from direct observation "out in the field" to the analysis of the health records of 53,000 Belgium people.

There have been reliable findings of associations between laughter and various conclusions (e.g., gender differences in laughing). But in many instances, we can't make the leap to causation. (e.g., The finding that laughter is correlated with longevity may be mediated by a third variable, e.g., people who laugh a lot may have better health care, resulting in longer lives.)

Never mind all of these reservations. It certainly won't hurt to reach for a little laughter every day. In the highly unlikely event that one of my grandchildren should ask for advice in finding a mate, as a model I would tell them to check out their grandmother, who got me on the first date and is still a world class laugher.

Feeling Good About Millennial Generation After Grandson's Visit

For the last two months we have had a member of the Millennial generation living with us. (I have written a little about this current generation but you will have forgotten about it.) The Pew Research Center has focused on it for about five years, and working on the thesis that generations have personalities, can now lay out some of the major characteristics. The researchers describe it as the most ethnically and racially diverse in the nation's history; the most politically progressive; the least religiously observant; more inclined to trust institutions than earlier generations.

Our grandson Sam, almost 21, is a junior at UC Santa Barbara and recently decided to take a quarter off. We invited him to stay with us and he just returned to California after two months in Tallahassee. It was an instructive experience for us, and possibly also for him.

Several days after his arrival we decided to go out for dinner, and Sam asked about dress. Betty said it was casual. When he appeared wearing flip-flops, shorts, and a t-shirt, Betty said that was not exactly her definition of casual. Within three minutes he returned, wearing pants, shirt, socks and shoes.

Betty and Kent with grandson Sam Theg

Shortly after we were seated another party was brought to an adjacent table, including a man who looked to be about 20, wearing flip flops, shorts, a t-shirt. Sam was smart enough not to call attention to him, but catching my eye said in a soft voice, "I think it's a generation thing." This was the first of a number of "generation things" as we learned from one another in the following months.

Sam found a job in construction, doing hard dirty labor and learning that was not something he would like doing for a living. He learned from me that I did not like him driving with two fingers of the left hand resting on the steering wheel while eating a breakfast bar with the other hand. And that driving while wearing flip flops causes a staggering number of accidents (flip flops double the time to move from gas to brake). He saw that there were occasional advantages to moving about with an old man, e.g., when exiting the arena following a basketball game, people will give way.

In turn, Betty and I learned, or relearned a few things we had forgotten, e.g., that a healthy 21-year-old can eat four times as much as we do. That indeed he was master of all electronic devices. There was no limit on energy (going with me to the gym at 6 a.m., working, and returning to the gym at 10 p.m. for pickup basketball). And given the chance, he was a world class sleeper.

Wanting to know more about this generation, I went online and found a questionnaire that purported to quantify (0 to 100%) just how much you were a true Millennial.

To give you a feel for things, here is a sample of the questions: In the last 24 hours have you watched television? In the last 24 hours have you read a daily newspaper? Do you have a tattoo? Should people of different races marry? How important is it for you to have a successful and high paying career? How important is a religious life for you? Were your parents married while you were growing up? In the last year have you contacted a governmental official?

As the result of our intensive time with Sam, we felt we could answer the questions as he would have. This exercise resulted in a score of 92%.

Yes. We know that the Millennials will grow older and change will occur. But at the moment we feel good about this generation.

(Sam, your departure has left a big hole.)

It Takes a Village to Get Best Health Care

Most days I delude myself into thinking that I am in relatively good health, taking only one or two prescription drugs. But it takes a lot of people to keep me moving. In 2014 I saw the following health specialists: neurologist, dermatologist, speech therapist, internal medicine, psychologist, and probably a half dozen more that I can't recall. I missed the ob/gyn, psychiatrist, hospitalist (the doc who takes care of you when you enter the hospital so that other docs don't have to make rounds there).

As an aside, I admit to a twinge of guilt over consuming so much of the available health care, and know what a privileged position I am in.

Specialization in medicine is here. (But I refuse to believe the rumor that there is an Atlanta hand surgeon who operates only on the right hand.) There are a lot of strangers treating strangers, a condition that will require a lot of hustle to make it work.

More than half of U.S. physicians now work in organizations that get their marching orders from insurance companies whose priority is a return on investment.

According to some studies, up to 80 percent of serious medical errors are related to miscommunication during transitions of care between all these health providers. The estimated numbers of serious errors are astonishing and run into hundreds of thousands.

What does all of this mean to us? That we need to be paying attention. Here are a few actions that might help.

Take someone with you for all contacts. It is amazing how competent people can hear radically different things.

Ask questions. Everybody is busy but most professionals welcome questions. if you have someone who doesn't encourage questions, try to find another professional who will.

Ask that a copy of everything, clinical notes, etc., be sent to your primary care doctor and to you. Take a card with your email address to hand them. Since everything is electronic, it is just a matter of a few keystrokes. It also means that inaccurate information can be easily removed. (Otherwise your significant other may not be able to even receive a phone call giving the results of a lab report.)

Betty recently found in the records of a physician's assistant, that she had been a victim of abuse. When she called she was told it was an error, and it was immediately removed. No harm done, but it could have had significant implications.

There is much more along these lines, but taking action on these three items above can carry you a distance.

Meanwhile, you might want to help us join the rest of the advanced western world in going to a single payer (Medicare for all) system. We are currently spending 14 percent of our Gross National Product on health. A simplified system of not-for-profit care would go far in reigning in the increasing fragmentation.

Sunday, May 3, 2015

We're All Touched by Emotional Contagion

A brief article in a recent news magazine caught my eye with the heading "Feeling Cold is Contagious." Researchers at the University of Sussex had subjects look at a video of a person immersing their hands in a vat of ice cold water with the result that the viewer felt cold all over and the temperature of their hands dropped a half degree. The researchers reported that this result was consistent with other reports of so-called emotional contagion.

I was not surprised by the report, but not familiar with the concept. A quick search revealed a mass of scholarly work (and some not so scholarly) going back 25 or so years. The basic notion is that being social animals we strive to understand the emotions of others, tend to mimic each other's vocalizations, posture, mannerisms, etc., all the while moving towards convergence of emotion. Non-verbal cues are important in this process, which is automatic and outside consciousness, making it possible to "catch" each other's emotions.

All of us know something about contagion. One baby in a room full of babies cries and soon all of them are crying. Spend time with a depressed person and you are not likely to leave whistling. One "up" person in a group can impact the entire group. Someone gives you a big smile and you smile in return. So, much of the research is a matter of confirming and quantifying the process and teasing out the specifics.

More recent research has expanded as businesses strive to make their customers happy and organizations want their leaders to share the same emotions. A recent study on Facebook demonstrated that emotional states can be transferred outside of personal contact. The researchers manipulated the amount of positive news feed to some 690,000 people, finding that a reduction of positive expressions led to reduced positive posts and a reduction of negative news feed increased positive posts. Neurologists, much on the scene everywhere, are tracking changes in emotional contagion as reflected in activation in the frontal cortex and parietal areas of the brain. Others have focused on emotional contagion in seduction and socializing.

I find some comfort in the number of people who are seeking empathy, convergence rather than divergence. And as messy as some of the research is, we are gradually adding to our knowledge about emotional exchanges, taking into account neurological functions, conditioning, and the role of cultural and sociological concepts. And we are making progress anytime we move the unconscious to the conscious.

Sunday, May 31, 2015

Blending in with Fads, Fashion in a 2015 Crowd

I say to Betty, "I'm planning to wear what I have on." She looks up from her book, pauses, and says, "Well, you'll look like everybody else." I got her drift, but the comment prompted me to consider what is happening in the world of style and fashion, usually a subject of limited interest to me.

We were scheduled to take a flight to California the next morning, which included transfers, an exposure to thousands of people. Herewith are a few of my summary impressions, sufficient to keep you from getting labeled totally "out of it."

On the way to the airport, I learned from *The New York Times* (May 22) that Kim Ky, J-Lo, and Beyonce undress for success, embracing the "naked look," which involves fanny-flouting and back-baring.

- Headwear of any kind is rare. I saw several baseball caps, but only two instances of the stupid practice of turning them backward. If you are looking for "cool," get one of those little fedoras that are coming on strong with both men and women. Shaved heads were not rare, and not restricted by age.

- Clothing (pants, jackets, etc.) tend to be slender, tight. Much of it looks as if it was constructed with materials that called for dry cleaning only and by error had been washed in hot water. (Pickpockets must hate this development. I need help to get my wallet out.)

- Mercifully, neckties are moving steadily towards oblivion.

- You can pay up to $220 for jeans with holes in the knees. Or, you can make your own holes with a cheese grater. (I lack the imagination to come up with an explanation for this.)

- The manufacturers of mesh, spandex, latex, are smiling on the way to the bank.

- My mother taught me that brown and blue clothes never go together. Today, anything goes, mixed patterns, mixed colors that I think of as garish.

- Overnight, men wearing their shirts outside of their pants is fashionable. At least I understand the reason for this: comfort and the disguising of a pot belly.

- Tattoos, everywhere, across genders. But not all are to be seen. The Leon County Sheriff's Department requires that all new tattoos be covered.

- Thankfully, the custom of sagging pants was not to be seen on this trip.

Enough already. This was an interesting exercise for me, making a three-hour plane delay pass quickly. This is what I saw. You would likely come up with a very different set of observations. Some of us want to melt into the crowd, others want to stand apart. Most would like a little of both. Some of us work at the presentation of self, knowing that it takes additional effort in the later years. While others say the hell with it, I have bigger issues on my mind.

Even so, there was remarkable homogeneity. It was clearly a 2015 crowd, not that of a generation ago.

Mysteries of Electricity Show Promise for Brain Repair

Have you talked to a neurologist lately? No? Live long enough and the bets are that you will, and you will find that they are doing some interesting things. In spite of the fact that they are essentially electricians.

What do electricians do? They drill holes, pull wires, insert metal here and there, modulate the strength of the power used, and work very carefully, knowing that the slightest misstep could be disastrous.

Just so for some neurologists. What they work with starts with that three pound (or less if you are old) hunk of meat we call the brain. Nothing happens unless some of the estimated one billion neurons can talk to one another (how do they get that count?) and that requires electricity.

I suspect most of you are like me, not giving much thought to the role of electricity in our lives. But what else can heal wounds, make it easier to butcher pigs, is used by the state to kill and take out suspects (taser), and lets a "frozen" Parkinson's victim walk again almost immediately after a single treatment?

In 1874, it was known that applying an electric charge to the brain would produce movement. By the early 1950s, when I was a graduate student working for the VA, electric shock therapy was a commonplace treatment for the seriously mentally ill (i.e. depression, mania, suicide, schizophrenia) who had not benefited from other treatments. ECT (electroconvulsive therapy) was controversial from the start, with the critical movie *One Flew Over the Cuckoo's Nest* having a significant impact.

Fast forward some 50-some years, to find a refined and expanded role for electronic treatment. e.g., ECT is now applied in short bursts, with the induced seizure lasting less than a minute. The patient is given a muscle relaxer and anesthesia, thereby avoiding side effects such as broken bones and memory loss.

In recent years, we have learned much about the functioning of different areas of the brain and this has led to neural implants involving deep brain and Vagus nerve stimulation. There are no hard numbers on the success of these treatments but clinicians estimate improved functioning about 50% of the time.

And there is no understanding of why or how it works. Some suggest the electricity breaks the rhythm of brain waves, somehow "resets" the function. Others speculate about the functions of certain neurons.

A dramatic example of the significance of specific areas of the brain was reported in the May 22 issue of the journal *Science*. Richard Andersen at the California Institute of Technology and his associates taught a paralyzed man to use nothing but his thoughts to control a robotic arm. Doctors implanted a pair of tiny chips into the brain of Erik Sorto, who was paralyzed 10 years ago.

These sensors recorded the electrical activity of his brain cells located in the parietal cortex and sent them to a computer. (Previous researchers used the motor cortex.) Soto was instructed to think of the movements he wanted to make – in this instance to bring a sip of beer to his lips, and the robotic arm did just that. It sounds a lot like black magic, moving an object across the room by nothing by thought.

Not everyone is eager to have holes drilled in their head, much less have metal objects stuck into the brain. But some will be willing to take the risk when all else has failed.

Budd Bell Was a Bulldog for Change

Some time ago, to commemorate the 100th anniversary of his birth, I wrote a column about Bill Bell, who was an FSU gerontologist. This one is about his wife, Budd Bell, social worker and activist whose 100th birthday occurs this month.

We learn from them that there are differing ways of having an impact on the lives of others and beating City Hall. I was a partner-in-crime with each of them, in differing ways: university stuff with Bill and downtown stuff with Budd.

During my 60 years in Tallahassee, we have had contact with exceptional people who committed a large part of their lives to improving the quality of life of others. I'm thinking here primarily of those concerned with justice and help for those in need, the poor, handicapped children, the disabled, the fragile elderly, the mentally ill. Budd was one of those people, going to the top of the list.

She came to Tallahassee in 1969, when she was in her mid-fifties, and in no time she was all over the town and the state and traveling to Washington to get money for Florida. She mentored hundreds of social work students; lobbied the legislature; helped in constructing the Baker Act (protecting the rights of the mentally ill). She fought for child care licensing, safety standards, and she brought to life organizations such as the Clearing House on Human Services to ensure the continuance of legislative programs. The Tampa Bay Times referred to her as the Conscience of Florida.

One measure of Budd's success was reflected in the number of honors that came her way. A complete listing would use up all the space for this column. And the honors came from politically diverse organizations.

How could she accomplish so much? Most of her time was focused as a volunteer, it was her job. When advocating, she knew her facts better than opponents. As a volunteer without a paycheck, she pointed out that she could say what she wanted. Receiving an award along with Rosalynn Carter in Tampa, she said, "It has been my pleasure to make trouble for the forces of evil in this state."

Budd worked hard. Convinced of the validity of her position she dug in and called out legislators and others who were on the wrong side of an issue, using her persuasive powers to change opposing positions. When needed, she would have the major players over for dinner and some of her apple and nut muffins.

It seems to me that Budd and others working in similar circumstances are sustained by a strong sense of purpose. She was a bulldog, tenacious, unwilling to compromise.

Those who knew her well also saw a soft side, a love of family, a desire to cuddle little children.

Bill worked quietly and systematically. Budd came prepared for open combat. They teach us that different styles can get you to the same place.

Even Families Grapple with Polarization

Last week I received an email from a friend (we will call him Joe) saying, "With a new political season rolling out, I suspect we will be on opposite sides of the coin..." Joe came into our life only a few years ago, by way of marriage into our extended family. He and I like one another, struck up a correspondence, hold a number of values in common. But there is a problem: Joe is a Republican.

In our extended family (sons-in-law, adult grandchildren, significant others, nieces, etc., totaling maybe 50 or 60 people) Joe stands out with only two or three other known Republicans. If there are more, they are surrounded by Democrats. Numbers like this are troublesome and certainly reflect something more than chance.

Evidence of polarization is easy to come by. Time and time again, legislators vote a straight party line. Judges come up with 5-4 decisions. Appointments rarely go outside party lines. Personal attacks are vicious and unrestrained. Any inclinations to "reach across the aisle" are squashed by the size of the aisle. I found strong evidence that what we perceive is indeed valid. Search the internet with "political polarization in U.S." and you will be taken to some interesting reading. One such is the Pew Research Center, a highly regarded organization, who reported in 2014 their findings based on interviews of 10,000 adults. Here is a sample of their conclusions:

- The overall share of Americans who express consistently conservative or consistently liberal opinions has doubled over the past two decades from 10% to 21%.

- Ideological overlap has diminished, with 92% of Republicans to the right of the median Democrat, and 94% of Democrats to the left of the median Republican.

- Many of those in the center stay on the edges of the political process, while the most ideological make their voices heard.

- Two-thirds of consistent conservatives and half of liberals say most of their close friends share their political views. (Shocking!)

- Two-thirds of conservative Republicans think the Democrats' policies threaten the nation's well-being. The corresponding number for the Democrats is 50%.

- Since 1994, highly negative views of the opposition party have doubled: 43% of Republicans; 38% of Democrats.

National Journal's Ron Brownstein says that the divide is not going to go away. Essentially, we have a durable standoff between a diverse, younger, urbanized, more secular Democratic coalition, and a predominantly white, older, non-urban and more religious Republican coalition.

No one knows how we have come to this point. Some suggest that partisan news media and the internet have helped. And it is not clear how to start dealing with the problem.

Most of us like to swim with people who swim as we do. It is natural to seek reinforcement by getting together with those who think as we do, who read the same columnists, even though we make token exceptions by reading a few columnists from the other side to get the juices flowing.

There are times when I feel that I should cut the Republicans a little slack. Then I conjure up the consequences if our next President is a Republican. There is a high probability that there will be two vacancies on the Supreme Court during his or her term. Adding another Thomas or Scalia would result in decades of untold damage to the search for justice and fairness. For me, this alone would be sufficient reason to see that it doesn't happen.

(Joe, we will talk.)

Travel Advice: Go for Aisle Seats, Extra Help

If you have read some of my columns, you know that I don't really offer much in the way of advice. Read on, for today I try to say something helpful about seniors traveling. The emphasis is on air travel, for I assume by now you know to avoid long trips by car.

First, you have to get the right mindset. If you want to be independent, you need to put on a face of competency, if you are troubled by appearing to be what you are — a fragile, needy old-timer, then you might as well go read your *Saturday Evening Post* now. Secondly, it helps to keep in mind that in accepting help you are providing people a way to feel good about themselves.

I was prompted to reflect on this topic by an incident reported by a friend. He belonged to a group that met regularly and had the custom of each person mentioning one good thing and one troubling thing that had happened. One of the participants said the good thing was that his parents were traveling in Europe. And the troubling thing? His parents are traveling in Europe, not on a tour, but on their own. Yes, lots of people seem to be worried about their elderly parents Traveling.

If you have any money at all, pay extra for the fewest number of connections possible. Yes, for the cheapest ticket to State College from Tallahassee you may have to fly 500 miles south to Miami (1,000 miles round trip). Not good for blood pressure, etc.

If you are flying from Tallahassee, you have to go through Atlanta, Charlotte, or Dallas, arriving at Terminal 2 and your connecting flight will be out of Terminal 26. Now Betty and I could probably make it, we have for years, but we have learned to order two wheelchairs. I travel with a big roll of $1 and as soon as we are seated I make sure the people pushing us see me take it out of my pocket. We have not failed to make the connection.

We fly with opposing aisle seats. Easy to get up and stretch, and if one of us draws a 300-pound seatmate or one that won't stop talking, we can share the misery by swapping. On a recent return trip from California, the stewardess greeted us with, "Hi! You came out with me last Tuesday, with opposing aisle seats." She seemed to remember replacing a pair of earphones that we had for 10 or 12 years. For reasons I don't understand, it seemed strange to her. Anyhow, she continued to put extra chips, nuts, etc. on my tray.

There is a high probability that at some point you will need some help, if for nothing else than the understanding of a garbled announcement or why all the people around you are suddenly getting up and walking away from their seats. Here is one of the most effective and easily mastered help getters. Stand in an open space where you can easily be seen. Just stand there. A blank expression. No movement except an occasional look up at a TV screen, or slowly turning your head over the shoulder. Within minutes and without fail someone will come to you to ask if you need help.

We have been surprised at how many good people there are. Even if some of them are motivated in part by feeling that they have not been sufficiently attentive to their parents.

Happy flying.

It's About Love, but Much of Happiness Is on Us

We don't know what inspired Thomas Jefferson to put into the Constitution the phrase regarding the right to pursue happiness. Just so, two hundred years later, we don't have a clear definition of the concept. Which doesn't slow down a massive industry working to uncover the correlates of happiness. Pollsters are out asking us to say whether we are very unhappy, unhappy, happy, very happy (pick one). Psychologists, historians, economists, and graduate students try to unravel the essence of what makes for happiness. There are books, a peer-reviewed *Journal of Happiness and Well-Being* and a stream of research reports. All of it dependent upon our individual assessments and what we are willing to say to strangers about our level of happiness.

Skimming across this material, I found a few things that floated to the top. (My fellow octogenarians face some special problems (e.g., dying), but by and large we are all in the same boat, not all that different from other age groups.)

Money still counts, with the rich being happier than the poor. But while income inequality in the U.S. has increased over the last 35 years, happiness inequality has decreased. Betsey Stevenson and Justin Wolfers of the University of Pennsylvania, found that the happiness gap between blacks and whites has fallen by two-thirds since the 1970s, the gender gap has disappeared. The unhappiest 25% of the population has gotten a lot happier, and the happiest quarter is less cheerful.

Richard Davidson's *The Emotional Life of Your Brain* contains evidence that happiness plays a significant role in long-term health. The author of *Happy People Live Longer*, reports that happy people live 14% longer, increasing longevity 7 to 10 years.

There are reports that richer nations are happier than poor. That the gay-straight happiness gap has declined. (The Supreme Court decision on marriage should help.) Studies of twins led researchers to conclude that happiness is 40% genetics, and 40% can be controlled.

There is a 75-year study that is worth pausing over. The Harvard Grant Study followed 268 students from the classes of 1938-1940, gathering data at regular intervals, teasing out factors leading to a happy life. (All of the subjects were male, Harvard not enrolling women until 1977. And Harvard students at that time were likely to differ from the rest of us in significant ways.)

Harvard psychiatrist George Vaillant directed the study from 1972 to 2004, and thankfully distilled 75 years of research into a handful of observations:

Love is really all that matters. It's about more than money and power. Regardless of how we begin life, we can all become happier. Connection is critical. The way we deal with challenges has a lot to do with shifting from narcissism to connection with others. (In Vaillant's words, the capacity to make gold out of shit.)

Dilip Jeste, of the University of California at San Diego, found similar results in a study of 500 Americans age 60 to 98, who lived independently with serious health problems. "In fact, optimism and effective coping styles were found to be more important to successful aging than traditional measures of health and wellness. These findings suggest that physical health is not the best indicator of successful aging — attitude is."

What's the takeaway from all of this? Much of life is in relationships, loving and being loved (not necessarily marital or romantic love). We are social creatures and need to be out and about. Much happiness comes in doing something for others. But happiness doesn't just happen. It is pretty much on our shoulders.

What, Me Worry? Lighten Up, Enjoy Life

If Alfred E. Neuman were alive he would be about my age. You will remember him as the snaggle-toothed icon on the cover of *Mad Magazine,* and more importantly for our purposes, he would still be embracing the phrase, "What, Me Worry?" Alas, he is a fiction, no help to us in how to reduce worrying about things not likely to happen or not worth the time. I am troubled (you might say obsessed) over the number of people approaching life negatively, rather than positively.

Most of us in our 80s need no help in finding things that are worrisome. But we overdo it, need to lighten up, and at this late hour should be seeking The Sunny Side of the Street. This is an auspicious time for doing so because so little is expected of us.

It might help to remind yourself that if you are reading this column, you are close to the top of the heap. You have a roof overhead, morning coffee, food, free time, clean clothes, and enough money for a subscription to the *Democrat.* In short, you have some control over what happens next.

If you feel slightly burdened, less than carefree, consider these steps: 1. Inventory the things that worry you. Put them in some rough rank order. 2. Identify those over which you have some control. Scratch the rest. 3. Remember that you are looking for joy. For example, no need to worry about offending friends and relatives by not being able to recall their names. Nobody expects you to and I have found that people usually introduce themselves with something like, "Hi. I'm Jim. I live three houses down the street."

Don't take anything I say here to imply that we should strive to be totally free of worry. It can be a force for good if it results in getting us to pay some attention to making things as easy as possible for those around us. For most of us, two issues are the major source of anxiety: health and final living arrangements (who will be taking care of us). Both of these demand whatever attention you can give.

And of course, you should continue to contribute energy and resources to whatever makes for a better world (you are not yet dead). Having done that, go find the fun. Find companions who laugh a lot. As you move through the day ask yourself "Is this fun?", "Does this TV program make me feel good?", "Is it fun to work in the yard?" If not, don't do it. And above all, don't spend much time worrying about all of this.

July 26, 2015

T-shirts and Narcissism: It's Ok to Bail

If I recall correctly, *Tallahassee Democrat* writer Bill Cottrell has disdain for columnists who use their platform to write about themselves. And somewhere I heard this quote attributed to *Democrat* writer Gerald Ensley: "Any man who goes out in public wearing a white t-shirt has given up." Well, here I am pleading guilty on both counts.

Several days ago I received in the mail a t-shirt emblazoned with a picture of Donald Trump and underneath 2016. There was not a clue as to the sender, but there was an invoice for $20 and postage was $6.25. I quickly exhausted the number of friends who would spend that much on a t-shirt for a joke. What in the world would I do with it?

Aha. I was planning to attend a Democrat Party gathering and thought it might elicit a laugh or two if I appeared wearing the shirt topped with this statement: Help can come from the damnedest places.

I went with a friend who knew about 90% of the crowd, making movement across the room a challenge because of introductions. Alas, only 4 or 5 people even noticed my shirt (but they did laugh heartily).

So here I was in my white t-shirt for the evening. Not my best presentation of self since it made me look scrawny and bent over. (I asked my orthopedic friend how much height can be lost over 80+ years and he said 3 or 4 inches.) Surely, those who knew me were convinced that I had turned the corner, given up.

My friend and I have been working together long enough that when I looked at him with raised eyebrows, he understood that I could leave any time. He signaled that we should wait at least until those at our table finished eating. We slipped out after the pledge of allegiance before candidates spoke.

Would-be writers are told they should write about something they know. Allowing for blind spots, I probably know more about me than almost anyone. Besides, most people want to know a little about the writer, it helps with the decision to read.

For my fellow octogenarians, here is what I take away from this little foray.

- Once again: Remember not to sweat the small stuff, and this certainly qualifies.

- Make better decisions about how and where you spend your time.

- Don't go to places where you can't hear or see. Send a check instead.

- Most of us tend to exaggerate the interest others have in us, what we are wearing, how we are looking, etc. In many gatherings, small and large, after a, "Hi, you're looking good", it is easy to become invisible.

- If you are out and find yourself wishing you were walking the dog or watching a game on TV, go do it.

Note: I have for sale a quality t-shirt, large, worn only two hours, to go to the highest bidder. They say politics makes strange bedfellows and the shirt would be good for sleeping. If I get no takers, I may do that.

It Takes Effort, But Staying Involved Is Rewarding

"Seth Miller to speak on the Innocence Project of Florida, sponsored by the Tallahassee Citizens Against the Death Penalty." The announcement evoked a feeling of been there, done that. And I am just settling into Alice Monroe's *Dear Life*. But once in a while I take the advice I so freely give to others. In this instance, I refer to the need to be out and about, in the presence of others, not yet folding the tent.

I reluctantly hitched a ride with friends and joined about 50 or 60 kindred spirits. Glad I did. There were exchanges with old friends, the meeting of new faces. And the insight that we must get some perverse pleasure in meeting with one another and agreeing things are going to hell. But there is also encouragement, hope, and support from such meetings.

The speaker was articulate and knowledgeable. His primary interest is on prisoners on death row who have been found to be innocent. In recent times there have been 150 exonerations nationally, with 25 of those coming from Florida. For every three executions, there is a prisoner found innocent. You would expect that those numbers would give pause to almost everyone, but state Representative Matt Gaetz wants to speed up executions.

One of the more important contributions from Mr. Miller was his take on the limitations of the various forensic tests used to determine guilt or innocence. (e.g., fingerprints, DNA, analysis of hairs, eyewitness testimony). He says that all of these are problematic, devoid of much of a scientific basis, and subject to manipulation. Add to that the findings that many confessions are false and coerced.

This is not the place for a detailed analysis of death row but there cannot be much doubt that Florida's numbers are among the worst in the country. And the U.S. has the highest incarceration rate of any Western nation. Death row is just the endpoint of a broken criminal justice system.

But there is reason for hope. An article in *The New York Times* (7/28/15) details developments at the federal level, drawing strong bipartisan support for change. The intent is to correct four decades of legislation that led to huge increases in the number going to prison and the length of time behind bars. The call for action is driven by both monetary and moral issues.

This could be a model for the states, some already moving for reform. There are signs that the death penalty is on the way out, just a matter of time.

The meeting I attended seemed long, as most of them do these days, and I take pleasure in hearing the moderator say, "Time for one more question." More often I'm not there to hear it. No reflection on the speaker.

If you have a little free time and some interest in learning more, you should drop in on the monthly meeting of TCADP (tcadp.net). You will be warmly greeted, meet some interesting people, and no one will ask about your politics.

A Few Drops of Wrong Thing Triggers Delirium

On a recent Friday morning, I woke with some strange feelings that I could not put a name on. I remember calling to wife Betty, "I need some help." That is all I remember of the next 24 hours, including an ambulance ride and an overnight stay in the hospital.

My family said that I was confused, hallucinating, disoriented, babbling nonsense. (OK. I know that some of my critics feel that is my default natural state, but I have a loving family.) Concerned that I might be having a TIA or a stroke, they called for an ambulance.

The hospitalist neurologist readily ruled out stroke. I am told that after listening to my responses to his questions, he asked the family if I always talked that much. (Apparently, I insisted upon answering each of his questions by starting with the Mayflower, gradually working up to my childhood.) He quickly identified a new prescription drug (new to me) as the source of my problems. Within 24 hours the drug had dissipated and I returned to my normal state.

I have zero memory of this entire event. The experience prompted me to read about delirium, a medical concept that has been around for many years. It is not a disease, but more of a syndrome with a number of signs and symptoms similar to psychotic and organic brain disorders. Characteristics: inability to focus attention and solve problems; sleep disturbances; agitation; slow and muddled thinking; temporal and spatial orientation impairment. It can wax and wane, frequently causing aggressive agitation.

Precipitating factors can include infections, post-traumatic stress disorder, aging, medication, sleep disorders, alcohol dependency, and much more. (On the positive side, long-term memories are usually preserved.) Delirium requires a sudden onset and an organic cause.

(Wikipedia is a good source for those wanting more information and references to scholarly papers.)

People are reluctant to talk about experiences like these, finding it embarrassing, but there are reasons to pay attention. Delirium hits hard with older people, with estimates that about one-third of patients over 70 experience "hospital delirium." It affects 10-20% of all hospitalized adults, 30-40% of elderly hospitalized adults, and much higher numbers for patients in intensive care units.

Malaz Boustani, research professor at Indiana University, said that delirium is "terrible, more dangerous than a fall." He notes that the disorder carries the risk of falls and much more. Pharmacologic management of delirium is a highly complicated process and patients are at risk for exposure to harmful medications.

I wound up with a clearer understanding of the damage to the brain that can come from just a few drops of chemicals. And a reminder that older people can't process dosage levels that younger people do. (We had a dramatic example of this with my father when at 82 he came to live with us. On his first morning, I found him in a coma. Our primary care physician immediately determined that the coma was induced by pain medication he had been given for a broken arm.)

You might mention some of this to your children. And if your medical chart contains the word delirium, take advantage of it. If you are asked to do something you would rather not, just say "Sorry. I can't do that. My old delirium you know." No one will challenge you.

(I am aware that some time ago I generously gave you "I can't do that. My old troubles, you know." You might alternate the two excuses, showing that you are still capable of learning new things.)

Sunday, September 27, 2015

Going to the Afternoon Movies Is a Treat

Betty loves the movies and likes to see all the coming attractions. Me, not so much. We have a little dance we go through each time. She says the movie starts at 3:30 p.m. and we should leave about 3:10 p.m. I respond that the actual movie doesn't start until about 4 p.m., I can drive us there in about eight minutes, and leaving at 3:30 p.m. should work. We have waltzed in this manner for 67 years and never would have made it if we had not been willing to compromise, as we did in this instance. We left at 3:10 p.m.

One of the benefits of being our age is the freedom to move about as we wish, including a movie in the afternoon. No lines, cheaper tickets, and the man selling them is the only visible employee.

When we arrived there were only seven people in the theater, so we could have sat where we could talk without offending. Another plus for an afternoon movie is that you are already wearing your leaving-the-house clothes (for me, long-sleeved, no wrinkle dress shirt and pants), so why not go out for supper? At 5:30, you can be assured of your choice of tables and the complete attention of the chef. If you had the foresight to bring along a book of love poetry to read to your partner while waiting for the food, you may have set the stage for a satisfying evening of romance, still leaving time for reading in bed until sleep by 10. Sorry, I digress. Back to the movie. As we got to our seats, we were hit with a blast of noise, and I said to Betty, "I can't stand this and I'm headed to the lobby." She suggested that it wouldn't last long and that I remove my hearing aids and clamp my hands over the ears.

One of the great mysteries in life is the national setting of the volume at a deafening level during the coming attractions. (Noise levels in theaters have been reported to exceed 110 decibels. Permanent hearing loss can occur at a single rock concert, and anything over 115 dB is never safe.) Many of the young are already hearing impaired and may need the extra volume. But in the absence of any rational justification for having the volume so high, I entertain the theory that managers of theatres must be sadists. (A movie chain in Virginia provides ear plugs and will give your money back if you leave within 15 minutes.)

The theater had just spent thousands of dollars on new seats that recline. They were generous in size and could be turned to a number of positions. But there was a problem. The room was totally dark and it was next to impossible to find the control panel. There were no instructions, it was a small smooth area like its surroundings, and when found, there was no way of knowing what to do next. Further evidence in support of my theory of sadism. (It is good to be able to report that among the seven of us in the theater there were two young people who saw us come in, assumed we would need help, and came over to provide it.)

At first, I thought the idea of reclining seats was silly. But as someone who is chronically short on sleep, it may be quite helpful. What could be wrong with catching a few zzzs?

When our extended family comes together I find that there are at least three topics of conversation that leave me out in the cold, movies being one. My children and grandchildren can recall the lives of actors, favorite movies they have appeared in, personal details. I like a good movie, can recognize Robert Redford and Marilyn Monroe, but that's about it. I have no interest in personal details, don't want to know who was the third partner, what book they are reading, their politics, or sexual preferences. This distancing makes it easier for me to accept them in the role they are playing on screen.

I learned from Betty that movies featuring older populations and venerable actors are on the rise (e.g., *A Walk In The Woods, Best Exotic Marigold Hotel, I'll See You In My Dreams, Quartet, Mr. Holmes*).

We've seen them all.

Enjoy.

Assisted Dying: Talk with Family About End of Life

At age 29, Brittany Maynard was diagnosed with brain cancer. She had treatment but the cancer returned and she was given six months to live. Deciding that death with dignity was her best option, she and her husband moved from California to Oregon, where the doctor could legally prescribe lethal drugs. She chose to die on November 1, 2014, having become the "new face" of the assisted dying movement, bringing into the light a highly debated subject.

In 2009, when Congress was considering the Affordable Care Act, Sarah Palin claimed that the intent was to establish "death panels" that would determine our fate based on a cost analysis. Her statements won the *St. Petersburg Times* fact-checkers Liar of the Year award. But she and her supporters were successful in their primary goal of stopping further expansion of the Affordable Care Act.

Skip on to 2015, when the Centers for Medicare and Medicaid announced a plan to pay physicians for counseling older patients about end of life options. While this plan was widely supported by a number of healthcare agencies, there was opposition from the

Catholic Church, Buddhists, and the American Medical Association. Supporters say there is a need to pay attention because of increased longevity if nothing else. (One reflection of this is the finding that 30% of all Medicare money goes to the last six months of life.)

This is the background in which Physician's Assistance in Dying (PAD) comes into play. Since this involves religious, social, ethical, and legal matters, controversy is inevitable. But the climate for PAD is much more favorable than it was in 2009.

Currently, there are 5 states with provisions for a physician to assist in accelerating death: Oregon, Washington, Vermont, New Mexico, and Montana. At least 18 other states are exploring legislative action, with support from national organizations such as Compassion and Choices, and Death with Dignity. Earlier this month the California legislature passed a bill that would allow doctors to help terminally ill people end their lives. If Governor Brown should veto the bill (his intent is not known), the issue would be taken to a vote of the people, with reason to believe it would pass. A Gallup poll in 2013 found that 70% of respondents favored physician involvement if the family and the person asks for it. Doctors have generally not favored giving assistance, although over the years some have given a prescription for a lethal dose. (The California Medical Association just changed their position to neutral). One survey found that over half of the doctors said they had received requests from their patients.

The experience in Oregon tells us that PAD would not result in an explosion of requests. Existing and proposed legislation comes with a number of safeguards: must be terminally ill; over age 18; written requests; approval of two doctors. Some states require the approval of a psychologist or psychiatrist. The California legislation requires a physician to meet privately with the patient, to ensure that no one is being coerced to end her or his life.

We need always to be on guard about the reach of government. But here we are talking not about more constraint, but giving the individual and family the right to make choices when the end is near.

Even if you are not interested in PAD, there are related issues that you should be working on with your doctor, and you may have to be the one to bring them up. Most doctors welcome such discussions, the opportunity to talk about options, to learn to what extent you want to continue with painful treatment that is problematic, etc. For example, you might want to consider ending life by refusing food and drink, a relatively painless exit that can take only 10 or so days.

Of course, gentle reader, thoughtful person that you are, you have already given this some thought and have a health directive. And surely you have talked with your family about what you want to happen/not happen. And they know where to find the papers. Better yet, you have given them a copy.

If I am wrong about all of this, it is later than you think and you need to get to work.

For Happiness in Old Age, Take Some Time To Have a Little Fun Today

We recently attended a party celebrating the 80th birthday of a long-time friend. It was a big party, lots of old friends, including many that we had not seen for years. Some had lost a spouse, some were currently caring for a mate with dementia and others were dealing with serious health problems. But in the face of all of this, there was an air of contentment and vitality that prompted me to look at what is known about the relationship between age and happiness.

A google search on this topic turns up more hits than you have time to read. A significant number point to evidence of an increase in happiness up until the 30s, followed by a dip until the 60s, when it turns up again. But with most subjects of this type, there are skeptics. Richard Easterlin, at Southern California, says there are some problems with the comparison groups, and, "When you take account of the fact that older people have lower income than younger, are less healthy and more likely to be living alone, then the old are less happy. Which is exactly what you would expect."

So. I think we can set this question aside and move on.

As life expectancy continues to grow, so too do stories about remarkable old people. A man who becomes a father at age 81. A woman writes a best-selling book, her first, at 84. The senior Olympics showcases old people breaking all kinds of physical records. Judges dispense justice well into their ninth decade. Some men get by without Cialis. A 94-year-old accountant works 30 hours a week and drives to the job. And so on.

What we see out of all this is a picture of a vibrant, competent, mass of elderly people. Unfortunately, most of us older people are not in that mass. On the other hand, expectations for us really old are so low that there is a certain freedom to act as we like. We can sleep any time we choose, feel no guilt over a game of gin rummy and coffee every afternoon or "wasted" time at the computer.

We can sit down and read anything at any time. Then there is the pleasure of surprising the family by dropping in conversation the name of Johnson's vice president in his second term. Did I mention how willing good people are to help you, give you a ride, pick up packages when they are out? In spite of all the troubles in the world, there is much goodwill about. I suggest taking a look at the obits each morning taking in the fact that your name is not there. Registering the fact that it is getting late and if you are to have some fun, or if there is someone you should write or a call you should make, it ought to be done today.

I know you can't totally follow this path. Freedom always comes at some cost. So spread some money around, find some cause you can endorse and give something of yourself. Somehow it all adds to the happiness quotient.

Fact Checkers: Getting to the Truth of the Matter

If you watched the recent debates by Presidential candidates you heard accusations, denials, he said/she said, lots of claims, backed up with contradictory statistics, etc. How do you decide what is factual?

Ideally, you turn to a fact checker. You probably have never met one, but there is a sizable industry of individuals and organizations devoted to doing the research to get to the truth. (A German weekly, *Der Spiegel*, is probably the world's largest fact-checking operation, employing the equivalent of eighty full-time workers.)

To get a feel for what they do we turn to the Democrats. Following the first debate, FactCheck.org came up with an eight-page summary of the falsehoods (lies) and misleading claims made by each of the candidates, along with details confirming the errors.

The lists were long, with similar findings for the Republicans. A quick scan of the reports failed to have much impact on my assessment of the debaters. In large part because they are politicians, and their primary purpose is to get elected. A little leeway in the heat of debate comes as no surprise and I am willing to cut them a little slack.

Not so for the news organizations. Look at this analysis by PunditFact in 2014. They used their news judgment to select which items to check, including statements made by a pundit, a host, or paid staffer. Each statement was rated as Mostly False, False, or Pants on Fire. Forty-five percent of NBC and 58% of MSNBC statements received one of the ratings above. The corresponding figure for CNN was 22%, and 58% for Fox and Fox News Channel. Scary?

A visit to Wikipedia Fact Check is simultaneously troubling and reassuring. At the top of the first page, there is an insert reading: "This article has multiple issues. This article needs additional citations for verification. Some or all of this article's listed sources may not be reliable."

All of this suggests that a certain amount of skepticism can be a healthy thing. Even with Science as our guiding star, that which we take as factual today may not be true tomorrow. For example, the Harvard Medical School is dramatically modifying its curriculum, in part because biomedical science and the practice of medicine is changing so rapidly. Dean Edward Hundert tells new students "half of what we teach you during your four years of medical school is going to turn out to be wrong or irrelevant by the time you graduate."

(This is not to degrade science in any way. When almost all climate specialists agree that global warming is caused by humans, it probably is.)

In searching for what is true there is a tendency to look to sources that we know will reinforce currently existing beliefs (not so for you and me, of course).

So. We need to identify the things were are sure of and hold the rest at a little distance. Trust your mother but cut the cards.

(This column has been fact-checked.)

Older Men Have Tougher Time Maintaining Friendships

The Wall Street Journal (yes, I read anything in the doctor's waiting room) of October 19 ran a story with this heading: "A Bonding Boom: More Guys Are Looking for Pals." And a subheading: "Typically men lose friends as they age. But now that's changing."

I was immediately reminded of a long-ago event. A friend asked me to join with him and some other men he named, to meet in the afternoon on a regular basis for talk or whatever. I liked the people and found it hard to say no. But our third meeting was slow starting, and sitting in silence for probably 20 seconds, in a low voice I asked, "Do we want to keep doing this?" There seemed to be overwhelming agreement, softened by the statement that maybe we could try again later. Without analysis, it just didn't seem right for a group of men to be sitting here in the afternoon talking.

The article in the WSJ contained a passing reference to the differences between men and women in making and keeping friends. I was skeptical and asked some of my friends and family attending a reunion last week what they thought and found that everybody seemed to believe the differences were significant. Older men have difficulty in making new friends while women readily construct social networks.

Almost any party you go to will quickly develop into a series of groups consisting of all women or all men, indicating some differences.

After a few hours at the computer, I came to several tentative conclusions. The similarities in friendships are greater than the differences, but there are some interesting differences. Ronald Riggio, writing in *Psychology Today*, summarized the current research. Men's friendships tend to be based on sharing activities (e.g., tennis, poker) or work-related projects. Women seem to share feelings, invest more time calling, meeting more often (frequently one-on-one). There is more physical contact, hugging, touching, etc.

One researcher asked men for the names and addresses of close friends, finding that these "close" friends had not been in touch for years and some were dead.

Perhaps one reason men go out to bars is that the alcohol allows them to drop some inhibitions and be more intimate.

Researchers give different weights to the role of brain structures, hormones, etc. as opposed to cultural factors. One study found that the type and quality of men's friendships were influenced by their parents' pattern.

Much of what I have said here is probably not a surprise. But we live in a time of rapid change and in a few years a column like this may be considered quaint. Still, there is a distance to travel. The millenniums, with their emphasis on relationships, may put on some finishing touches.

Now, back to the men's group sitting in my living room. The outcome might have been quite different if I had suggested getting a project to work on together.

Limited Expectations Hurt More than the Words

"Would a rose by any other name smell as sweet?" Perhaps. But names can exert forces that are outside our awareness. When subjects were asked which of two paired letters are preferred, there was a significant liking for letters which occurred in their name. There are a disproportionate number of dentists named Dennis, and men named Charles living in Charleston. A study of baseball players who died before 1950 revealed that players with positive initials, (e.g., ACE) on average, lived 13 years longer than those with negative initials (e.g., DED). Students with popular names such as David or Jennifer received significantly higher grades than those with unattractive names. No one says who decides which names are unattractive.

With this in mind, we turn to the words used to refer to the elderly. A few readers have suggested that I not use the word "old", or some other word they found unacceptable. But I have been surprised by the size of the passionate debate that is taking place over what this oldest age group should be called. There are conferences, polls to identify winners and losers, guides for the media. Here is a partial list of designations: elderly, golden ager, older adult, aging adult, senior citizen, older American, mature American, retired person, aged person. (And yes, there is another list: old folks, biddy, fogie, declining years, past sell-by date, winter of life.)

While I can affirm the significance of the words we use, I just can't get too upset. Yes, when the clerk at the checkout counter greets me with, "How are you doing today young man", I know that he is expressing ageism, a stereotyping. If I called him on it, he would not understand, feeling that he was just being friendly, so I give him a pass. (Meanwhile, I will try to be more sensitive and search for words as neutral as possible.) There are bigger issues that need attention.

Besides, the basic problem is not the words. It is the broader impact of ageism, a form of social discrimination, focused on decay and loss. Which is certainly there for all of us, much worse for some than others. But there are balancing freedoms and pleasures.

Even the young old (65-75) don't want to be cast in with the old-old, with their perceived greater physical problems and functional impairment, thereby categorizing what is actually a diverse people. While it is true that at some point we will all die, the timeline varies with each individual.

The fact that society holds such limited expectations of us, means that we should take responsibility for keeping things moving in our own lives.

It may be helpful to have some daily ritual or action to remind yourself of what is important: meditation, deliberate mindfulness, some form of exercise.

The fastest growing group is the over-age-80. Now, if we can just get organized there is still power in numbers. And the fact that we spend a lot of money, making our contribution to the GNP, should not be overlooked.

It's a Fine Line: Confidence or Narcissism?

In the 1940s school football players probably were as competitive as they are today. (Not as well coached.) But their style was something else. After a spectacular catch or run, walking back to the lineup the player could expect a pat on the butt and maybe a "nice catch." With a big smile on his face, he might say thanks. Cool.

Now skip to today, when such a play typically results in self-aggrandizing behavior: the man runs out of the crowd of players so he can be seen, does a little stylized dance that you and I could not possibly emulate, completes a chest bump with a teammate, points to himself and points up to God for helping him, possibly throws in a little trash talk.

In comparison with the 1940s, you have to admit this sounds a lot more interesting. But there is a problem lurking in the background: narcissism.

Currently, we are seeing a new focus on the subject, with new books published this year, and psychological tests designed to detect narcissism showing that scores in the U.S. increased every year since 2000. (A 2007 review of the literature listed the following "basic ingredients" of narcissists: think they are better than others; self-views tend to be greatly exaggerated; perceive themselves to be unique and special people; research supports the case for their being selfish; oriented towards success.) There is a long list of traits that expands on the above characteristics. Examples of narcissism are easy to find but it was two public figures that recently caught my attention.

As I write, Donald Trump, candidate for the Presidency, has doubled the support of his closest rival. Aside from a few throwaway proposals, his campaign is based solely on him, his personality, what he claims to have accomplished, a "Trust me, I am the only one that can get the job done," attitude. He has much to say, with no concern for the truth. The perfect narcissist.

The second figure is FSU's running back, Dalvin Cook. An article in the *Tallahassee Democrat* contained this quote: "I feel like I'm one of the great running backs in collegiate football." And in answer to a question, he said he thought he should win the coveted Heisman trophy. Indeed, he is highly talented. I am not dissing him, because his comments reflect contemporary norms. That's where we are.

(Note that a positive self-image is a good thing. Not much will happen unless you have enough confidence in yourself to do what is necessary.)

I can easily be dismissed as just an old man hanging on to yesterday. But it seems to me that all of us have enough failings so that it behooves us to invoke modesty. Not every thought has to be expressed. Not every act has to be applauded.

Now, in closing I would like to tell you a few things about me...

Meditation Flexes Your Grey Matter

Imagine this. You come across an activity that brings about changes in the anterior cingulate cortex, insula, temporoparietal junction, and the fronto-limbic network. But some of you might want more.

This activity is said to do the following: have a positive effect on attention, memory, verbal fluency; ease chronic pain; increase cognitive flexibility; help in the prevention of psychosomatic disorders; possibly increase longevity; change the brain in a positive way; lower blood pressure; ease musculoskeletal disorders, respiratory diseases and dermatological problems; support the immune system. And more. (No, it will not paint your toenails.) Topping things off, it costs very little and you maintain control.

Meditation is the subject. It has been around for ages, with much of the effort evolving from religious organizations. An emphasis on the spiritual life continues to some extent, but there is a broad mixture of types of meditation, something for everybody. Within the last 25 or so years, a significant emphasis on research has evolved, but this is very much a work in progress.

Each of the benefits in the second paragraph above has some support from the science world. But many of these findings will not hold up over time, suggesting that others should be lightly held. The concepts involved are complex, sample sizes are too limited, the measuring instruments fall short in terms of reliability and validity, and there are wide differences across the types of meditation. But the potential impact of understanding what gives with meditation is significant, particularly for the older generations. Patients with Alzheimer's often retain a spiritual consciousness and despite memory loss can benefit from prayers and related activities. This, in turn, was found to increase feelings of self-value and belonging. An article that covered 25 years of research confirmed that nursing home occupants can gain social and emotional benefits from meditation.

But the current interest in meditation is driven primarily by the younger generations. We are not aware of any of our peers that are involved. We do know of people who systematically set aside time for reflection, prayer, mindfulness, focusing on the given moment. These actions are similar to the more structured meditation in the shared intent to slow things down and encourage reflection.

In this context keep in mind the basic fact that across the board our expectations define how things play out.

Anyone in Tallahassee interested in further exploring this topic can easily find help online. The cost/benefit ratio is favorable.

Falls Among Elderly Not to Be Overlooked

"I have fallen, and I can't get up" was a catchphrase in the 1980s and 90s, based on a television commercial for a medical alert system. It was aimed primarily at seniors living alone who might fall and not be able to reach a phone. The commercial was unintentionally campy and badly acted, making it the subject for comedians, and giving it a place in pop culture. (In the same commercial an elderly man named Mr. Miller, no relation to me, popularized "I'm having chest pains.") Just 30 years later this kind of joking about old age is highly unlikely. Too many falls with serious consequences. Many of you reading this column will have experienced a fall or seen the problem in their aging parents.

A cursory visit to the Center of Disease Control yields some scary developments: one-third of the people over 65 fall each year and at age 80 the figure jumps to over half; falls are the leading cause of death due to injury and those who fall are two or three times more likely to fall again; falls account for 25% of all hospital admissions. Men are much more likely to die from a fall. Because many falls are not reported, these figures are probably conservative. The numbers should prompt us to pay some attention, particularly in light of the belief that many falls are preventable.

In the face of all of this, some of us embrace denial. One out of three adults age 65 and older falls each year, but less than half talk to their healthcare providers about it. Reluctant to transition to a cane or walker, or even wearing a pendant. We might tend to shade our response when seeing a neurologist whose first question is usually when was your last fall? Many people who experience a fall restrict their activities out of fear, further increasing the probability of another fall. There are a number of actions that can help. I will rank order my opinions.

- Exercise is the single most beneficial thing you can do. Get a referral to a physical therapist and follow directions. Stay with the program until you are sure that you are doing the exercises appropriately. If you need the discipline of a fixed schedule, try a trainer or group exercises.

- Get a review of all medications (prescription and non- prescription). Most elderly people are taking a number of medications, with the likelihood that some of them are working at cross-purposes.

- Be sure that vision is as good as possible by annually checking with your eye doctor. Ensure good lighting throughout your home.

- Work on your environment. Checklists are readily available from your health care provider or online. Suggestions range from the elimination of loose rugs, good lighting, railings, non-skid shoe soles, to painting the toilet seat black with a wide white circle around it.

- It would not hurt to see that you are getting adequate supplies of calcium and vitamin D.

I hope this doesn't fall on deaf ears. Good luck.

The Problem Isn't Information Overload, It's Failure to Filter

Was it yesterday or the day before that you complained about information overload (IO)? So much information bombarding you that making decisions is next to impossible. Drowning in a sea of words and numbers. Feeling guilty for not being able to assimilate it all, while knowing that there are limitations to what our brains can store and retrieve.

This is not a new concept, having been described hundreds of years ago, but recent electronic advances feed the beast in startling ways. I just googled the phrase and got 14,500,000 results in .67 seconds, for whatever that is worth. And two-thirds of adults are said to have smartphones, busily generating more IO.

In all of this hand-wringing and writing there seems to be an assumption that we are all spineless idiots, incapable of changing our behavior, leaving the phone off, finding the delete button, closing the office door for a few hours, not checking email every twenty minutes.

In his book *The Information Diet*, Clay Johnson uses the metaphor "eating the dessert first", referring to the tendency for people to consume information that they find interesting. His comment reminded me of an incident I witnessed in a cafeteria, in which a woman pushed her plate of food to the side, and ate her pie first. I admired her for thinking and acting against the rules when there was no harm to others.

I am in agreement with the observer who said the problem is not IO, it is filter failure. I will illustrate my attempts at filtering by focusing on the *Tallahassee Democrat*. We have subscribed to it for 61 years and I still find pleasure in walking out to pick it up between 4 – 4:30 a.m. (not many distractions). It is traditional to knock the local paper, and I have joined in on occasion. But I would hate not having it. Even on days when pages 1 and 2a are devoted to something like how Tallahassee is becoming the world beer capital.

- Before sitting down, throw away all inserts (except the Publix ad), the classified section, real estate, whole pages devoted to pictures of cute children and animals, gardening, movie reviews, wine and dining.

- For years, the sports section was my first read. Now it is the last – three minutes. I just don't care anymore (except for the Noles).

- I dropped the funnies many years ago. Not funny, and beyond my understanding of why they are there. (Almost as puzzling as what the *Democrat's* Storytelling Coach does. Do we need one in Tallahassee?)

- The full page listing a news story from each state holds no interest for me.

- Rather than scanning the pages of the obits I go to the Death Notices to see if I knew anyone on the list and whether they were older than I am.

- There are certain regular columnists that I used to read in order to keep up with what the other side was thinking. Skipped them when I realized that they had nothing new to say.

That's my filter and I am sure yours would be different. I follow the same pattern with the other subscriptions that come to us - *The New Yorker, The Nation, The Week,* various newsletters, professional reports, etc. Not much IO for me. Or for most of those in my age bracket.

You are not a helpless idiot. And on occasion, you too should feel free to eat the pie first.

Can Body Language Change Our Minds?

In 2012, Amy Cuddy, a social psychologist, gave a TED talk that was the second most popular ever (28 million viewers). It was titled "Your Body Language Shapes Who You Are" and led to a 2015 book: *Presence—Bringing Your Boldest Self to Your Biggest Challenges.*

Presence is defined as the opposite of powerlessness, believing and trusting yourself. But many of us are anxious, doubting our competence, feeling like a fraud, worrying about what others are thinking about us, rather than what we think about our self. And all of this is reflected in our body language, which can be altered by assuming power postures. For example, feet spread out, hands on hips, shoulders back, head held high. Simply assuming such a posture makes you feel different and provokes physiological changes, i.e. an increase in testosterone (dominance hormone) and a drop in cortisol (stress hormone). All from just assuming a particular posture. Give a police investigator a larger chair (increased power?) and you get better results.

Cuddy is a social scientist and supports her conclusions by reference to current research. One viewer said that the first part of the book reads like an academic review of the literature. She has been remarkably successful in gaining an audience and testimonials to her helpfulness.

The idea that body language and the way one presents his or her self to the public makes a difference, is not an altogether new concept for most of us. We understand that when we have new clothes, a pleasing hairstyle, have lost 20 pounds, we feel more powerful and can handle the world. What we expect in life is frequently what we get.

I have not seen any data on the age of those who have responded to *Presence,* but I suspect there were not many elderly. All of us would like to dump the anxiety, fears, etc., that are part of life. But I think that my age peers are not worrying much about being more powerful. Sure, all of us would like a little respect, and we know that the presentation of self makes a difference. But it takes some effort to see that breakfast is not showing on the clothes, socks match, teeth are free of spinach, and shirt buttons are aligned.

I leave you with a few observations and a confession. I am still surprised at the number of people searching for help in gaining power, reducing anxieties and fears of daily living. Paying attention to body language may help with self-image but no amount will carry the day. What people really want is acceptance, love, competence, a compassionate community.

Once again, I am impressed by the complex exchanges between our behavior and the brain. We are just scratching the surface.

Confession: I could not lay my hands on the book and have not read it. A surprising amount can be learned from reviews.

Sunday, February 7, 2016

Help Chase Away the Dark Clouds

This curse seems to be hanging over our heads. People are on edge, enough so that they turn to Donald Trump for relief. In my 60 years of observing Florida politics, I have never seen the left and right further apart. The sky is falling.

In Florida, the Republicans have a 2:1 edge in the Senate and the House, as well as the Governorship. Still not happy. They fight about this and that, pick up their marbles and go home in the middle of a session. The governor sits off to the side singing his two-note song: cut taxes (destroy government) and create jobs. Over the years, when the legislature was coming to town, one could hear cries to "Lock up everything. Nothing is safe." I was reminded of this when reading a recent comment from Florida Sen. Chris Smith (D) about the difficulties of representing his constituents: "As long as the bills are still filed we could see them brought up on day 59. As long as we are in session we will continue to sound the alarm because we are not safe from the Legislature."

This context makes it easy to distance ourselves from the political scene. The sense of powerlessness increases when you know that most of the heavy lifting in getting a budget, which drives everything else, takes place in the dark. Finally, if you are anywhere near our age, the

Kent and Betty at the Women's March in Washington, D.C., April, 2004

entries in your calendar lean heavily towards medical appointments. Being old takes a lot of time, a lot of time to get there, a lot of time to stay there. The stakes are high and somebody needs to be riding herd. As long as we are alive we have some reasonable chance of making it a better place. You can talk to your neighbors, write op-eds, make phone calls, and spread a few dollars around at the end of the month.

Here are a few of the hundreds of issues that may be considered in this session: school vouchers, death penalty, gun control, incarceration rate, fracking, mental health. Investigative reporting by newspapers is in decline but the internet is alive and well. (Take note that it was a *Tallahassee Democrat* reporter, Jeff Burlew, who broke the Solix story, in which a private company got 71 percent of the money it collected for a state employee charitable campaign.)

As we struggle to do our best there are some background factors that need to be kept in mind:

Polarization is a reality. Liberals and conservatives are on edge, disagreeing not only on what the problem is but how to fix it.

No political party can lay claim to purity. We are critical of the Conservatives in Florida because they are in control. But I recall the Pork Choppers of the 1950s and '60s, who gave us some of the worst times in Florida history (civil rights violations, witch hunts for gays and communists, etc.).

Personal attacks and expressions of hate won't help your cause. A little more civility might.

Maybe we have taken a few steps forward. The Dozier School for Boys, a longtime reform school in northwest Florida, is back in the news with another report from researchers. Some 50 to 100 boys died and were buried on the grounds. Several men who were boys in the school said they saw boys beaten to death. I like to think that such abuse would likely not happen today with the media outlets for whistleblowers. Come join them. The sky is not falling, just a few dark clouds.

Question: Why Do Scientists Cheat?

Question for the day. Why do scientists cheat? Answer: Most scientists are human and motivated by the same forces that cause the rest of us to cheat. It is easier than working, we want fame and fortune now, and for some, there is a twisted satisfaction in getting away with something. The specifics differ. The scientist is also subject to the "publish or perish" dictum, and the more papers with his or her name, the better.

Most of you reading this column go about your lives with a basic faith in science without giving it much thought. We assume that the expensive pills we take have been shown in the lab to be effective, that the moon is not made of cheese, that the data support the reality of global warming. Even the non-scientists are aware of the basic requirements of science: replication, peer review, transparency. However, most scientists are not particularly interested in repeating others' research and prefer to focus on their own. Thus the requirement of replication often gets by-passed.

Those who argue that cheating by scientists is rapidly expanding, point to several developments: reviewers are missing red flags; investigators are manufacturing numbers; refusing or unable to provide basic data; authors are guilty of plagiarizing. Scandals have hit some of our most distinguished universities, ending in broken careers (e.g., Marc Hauser at Harvard was accused of fabricating data on his studies of the cognitive behavior of monkeys. Karen Ruggiero, Harvard Psychology Department, was guilty of fabricating five experiments which had been published in two articles.) On a recent anonymous questionnaire, 2 percent of the scientists admitted to fabricating or falsifying data and 14 percent had seen such behavior from one or more of their colleagues.

Retraction Watch, an independent blog, reported that in their first year they found approximately 200 retractions (editors having to remove an article because of some form of cheating).

It is difficult to say whether the incidence of cheating is rising or whether we are better at finding it. Certainly, there is more out there. But I have spent a lifetime in the academic world, including time at the National Institute of Justice and the National Institute of Mental Health, without seeing cheating. A more challenging problem for social scientists is the tendency to look for data which supports a pre-existing belief or ideology, and ignoring that which does not.

What are the implications of all of this? The existing structures for oversight should be supported and cheating should continue to be much easier to spot. We already know that about half of what we consider to be solid science today will not be so in a few decades. This should cause us to retain a little skepticism. Still, science is the best thing we have. And skepticism guards against the problem that what we expect is likely to be what we get, because the placebo effect is strong.

Whistling: A Time-honored Tradition

I have whistled on and off since adolescence, as most boys did, never giving it much thought. Even though I don't have an ear for music, I can do a fair job at "I Don't Want To Set The World On Fire."

By and large, whistling for me was associated with a happy mood; relaxed, fooling around. It is almost impossible to whistle when you are unhappy. But if you could force it, perhaps it could help with the unhappiness. I thought about this recently when seeing a speech therapist who was giving me some exercises to strengthen certain facial muscles. I asked if whistling would help. Indeed, yes. Which led me to a Google search, as I am prone to do when wanting a little more information on a subject.

It occurred to me that I had not heard much whistling recently. Had it dropped out of vogue or was it just that I was not getting out of the house as much? If it is not now cool, when and why so?

Wow. I quickly learned that my vision of a low-key, pleasant activity, just on the edge of unconsciousness, was not shared by everyone.

People fall on a continuum from liking, to tolerating, to hating. The hate group is significant in number and depth of feeling: "I want to grab his head and slam it against the wall," "I would like to punch him in the mouth," "When I hear her I want to smash furniture."

Websites are full of postings such as these and there is even a sound disorder, misophonia. Individuals with this problem have a hatred for specific sounds, whistling being one of them for many, which cause negative emotions, thoughts, and physical reactions. I never whistle in elevators or other close places, but in my ignorance, it is likely that I have offended some and hereby ask forgiveness.

Scanning across articles it was apparent that whistling is a male thing. Why? Women have the same basic structure for whistling that men do. The answer has to be sexism. Betty reminded me of a saying she learned as a girl: "A whistling woman and a crowing hen will never come to any good end." Note that for a woman to whistle on a boat meant bad luck. Sailors believed it would increase the wind.

Superstition relating to whistling has been common across cultures. Do it indoors and bring on poverty. Do it at night and attract bad luck, bad things, evil spirits. Transcendental whistling would summon supernatural beings, wild animals, and impact the weather. Powerful stuff.

If you want to hear an expert, go to Whistlin' Tom and get some of his work. Key West is his home when he is not out touring the world with his three-octave range, whistling on both the in and out breaths.

In closing, I call attention to the annual International Whistlers Convention in Louisburg, N.C., which has awards for males and females, and for children of all ages. To honor the art of whistling, the Governor annually declares "Happy Whistlers Week." Go have some fun.

Sex in Old Age Just Another Fact of Life

For my parents' generation, death was not a topic for discussion. Currently in Tallahassee, you can join a group that meets weekly for that purpose. Just so with sex. Erica Jong, author of the novel *Fear of Flying*, now 73, talks about the pleasure of looking at a beautiful young man and not everybody thinks it is unseemly for a woman her age to write about longing and lust. Diana Athill, London book editor, age 98, writes "What I was really happy with was a lover who had a nice wife to do his washing and look after him if he fell ill, so that I could enjoy the plums of love without having to munch through the pudding." Explicit scenes involving seniors and sex abound on TV and on film. (Some of us might not be ready to go as far as the French movie *Love,* in having young actors have real sex instead of the simulated sort.) And most of you will get this joke: A seven-year-old boy was asked what he knew about the resurrection. "I don't know much, but if it lasts more than four hours you should see a doctor."

Elderly sex is pretty much out in the open. One factor that drives interest in old timers is that there are so many of us. In 1930 only 6% of the U.S. population was over age 65, but by 2015 the corresponding figure was 15%.

In 2013, I wrote a column on aging and sexual activity, concluding that many seniors are active well into their 70s and 80s. Research on these topics has steadily improved in quantity and quality, now involving mainline journals and social scientists. What we are learning is still heavily dependent on self-report, but other objective sources are being brought into play (e.g., rate of sexually transmitted infections in nursing homes and other residential living communities). Keep in mind the distinction between correlation and causation, with most of the research correlational.

Researchers have identified a number of characteristics that are associated with an active sex life. Here is a sample: protects aging brain (Reuters.com); men have a higher desire, fantasize more, and think about sex differently (International Longevity Centre). Sexual activity is said to reduce stress, improve sleep, strengthen the immune system, improve memory, and increase longevity (Reuters.com). Why are you still sitting there reading?

Another recent development is a broadening of the definition of sexual. In the words of one writer, "there is more to sex than the old "in-out." Results from an important study of 806 older women in California led investigators to this statement: "In this study, intercourse was not always necessary for sexual satisfaction. Those who were not sexually active may have achieved sexual satisfaction through touching, caressing, or other intimacies developed over the course of a long relationship." (Broader findings from this study were published in the January 2011 *American Journal of Medicine* under the title "Sexual Satisfaction in Women Increases with Age.")

All this tells us we are learning a few things. One of them is that as strong as the sex drive is, it is intimacy that we want. And I suspect that many people of advanced age have come to satisfactory terms with their sex life independently of what others may or may not be doing. Just as it should be.

Recall the Benefits and Power of Civility

I recently came across a reference to "The Disgust Scale," which piqued my curiosity. The website invited me to give them a little information about myself and see how I scored. There were 32 items like these: It would bother me tremendously to touch a dead body; If I see someone vomit it makes me sick to my stomach; It bothers me to hear someone clear a throat full of mucus.

In an op-ed titled "Would You Slap Your Father? If So, You're a Liberal," Nicholas Kristof writes that conservatives are more likely to perceive disgust and are distressed by actions that are disrespectful of authority. Liberals are not troubled as long as Dad gave permission to be slapped. He concludes from this and other studies, that liberals and conservatives feel and think differently. Many of these differences center on contrasting views of the proper role of government.

Americans have always had a love/hate relationship with central government, with an emphasis on hate. President Reagan had a storehouse of quips: "If the government made road signs that were too short, it would correct the problem by lowering the road." "Government is like a baby. An alimentary canal with a big appetite at one end and no responsibility at the other."

And every spring we hear the exact hour when we can "quit working for the government and start working for ourselves," meaning that until that hour the wages of the average American would have gone for taxes. The statement implies that all the schools, libraries, roads, police, fire departments and social services received from the government should be discounted and that the government is an alien entity sucking up our money without benefit to us.

In the context of this anti–government feeling it is worth noting that 70 percent of federal tax money goes to four programs that most Americans regard as untouchable: defense, debt reduction, Medicare, and Social Security (these figures are from a few years ago). As of January 1, 2016, only 22 percent of our gross national product goes to government. And a considerable chunk of money gets transferred to corporate welfare, privatization, and the top 1 percent. We need to continue to call attention to these issues. And we need organizations like the ACLU when government oversteps into our private lives.

I write here to my old brothers and sisters and those about to be old (boomers) hanging around in senior centers, retirement communities, and nursing homes (about 5 percent). As the fastest growing segment of the electorate (30 percent over age 65 by 2030), we need to be aware that we can make a difference.

In recent years, a lot of attention has been given to generational differences in liberal/conservative preferences, usually finding the youngest segment to be more liberal and the oldest more conservative. Things are more complicated than that, but the older segment has more impact on elections. A 2016 Pew Research Center found that "25 percent of adults 65 and older were closely following the midterm elections, compared with 5 percent of adults ages 18-29."

Not a good time to grab the reins. There are no clear paths out of this mess, especially in light of what may be the most severe polarization in our lifetime. But we can do our part with civility and politeness. Pundits suggest we have to start at the individual level, making contact with the opposition, eating together, listening to one another, searching for common ground where it can be found. We have to go beyond the tendency to look only for that which confirms what we already believe.

We will survive by loving this country and not going to Canada regardless of the outcome of this election.

To Combat Loneliness, Find Something to Love

"When so many are lonely as seem to be lonely, it would be inexcusably selfish to be lonely alone." - Tennessee Williams

Researcher Tim Smith says that measured over a century's time, more people are living alone than ever before. The rising rates are reason enough to try to understand what is happening. Are these people living alone lonely? Not always.

We are dealing here with a complex concept, and all of us at one time or another have had fleeting thoughts of being on the outside, with no one close, being apart from others. These feelings can come when alone or in the midst of a crowd. They can be provoked by the loss of someone close (whether by death, divorce, work, travel, etc.). Some who are subject to depression have strong feelings of loneliness. In the midst of this, there is research suggesting that as much as half of the measurable differences in loneliness are driven by genetics.

A recent article by Smith and his colleagues at Brigham Young University was based on reviewing years of research. A major conclusion was that loneliness cuts longevity and impairs health. They liken loneliness to obesity and smoking 15 cigarettes a day, as well as a number of health markers (e.g., high blood pressure, elevated cortisol). The incidence of reported loneliness is about 25 percent or 30 percent, particularly among the elderly and people living in low-density suburbs.

Another recent meta-analysis failed to confirm the relationship to longevity but supported the findings on health. Both reports were published in peer-reviewed journals. The differences probably came in large part from different criteria, controls and age groupings. (Recall that I said we are dealing with complex stuff.) There are some objective measures of loneliness, but much of the research is based on, "If you say you are lonely, you are lonely."

On a positive note, loneliness has given birth to some excellent poetry (Emily Dickinson), music and art.

What advice is out there for the lonely person wanting to take action? Same old stuff. Get exposed. Take the risk of making contact at public meetings, lectures, etc. Get a dog you have to walk. Get a few sessions with a therapist. Group therapy is even better. Keep contact with friends and family out of town by Skype.

Give some thought to bigger changes, like moving. If your job requires long commutes, explore other work. (You don't need all that time sitting by yourself in a car.) Consider moving to a retirement community where folks have daily contact at meals and gatherings that assuage the loneliness of those living into old age. I know that many of these options may well not be available for you, but you get the idea.

I recently came across the following quote from Mother Teresa:

"When Christ said 'I was hungry and you fed me,' he didn't mean only the hunger for bread and for food; he also meant the hunger to be loved. Jesus himself experienced this loneliness. He came amongst his own and his own received him not, and it hurt him then and it has kept on hurting him. [We have...]the same hunger, the same loneliness, the same having no one to be accepted by and to be loved and wanted by."

I endorse her understanding that loneliness at its deepest level is an expression of our need for affirmation and love. Lonely? Find something to love and give yourself to it.

Scientists Messing with the Brain

In the summer of 2015, the journal *Science* contained an article describing how a paralyzed man used only his thoughts to control a robotic arm. Two California doctors had implanted small chips in his posterior parietal cortex, bypassing a damaged spinal cord. On his first effort to bring a beer to his lips, he spilled it. The second attempt was successful.

This is just one example of a surge of interest in brain functioning. (An estimated 100,000 people in the U.S. have had some kind of implant.)

My first exposure to what I call messing with the brain (MWTB) was when I was an undergraduate in college (late '40s) and learned about happenings in the Eastern State mental hospital in Williamsburg. Electroconvulsive therapy (ECT) was applied by strapping the patient on a gurney, electrodes were placed on the side of the head and a blast of electricity shot through the brain, evoking massive contractions, some broken bones, and not much good.

My second exposure to MWTB came several years later from my work at the VA mental hospital in Waco, Texas. On my first day, while walking across the grounds, I passed a number of inmates who had similar "blank," non-expressive faces. They had undergone frontal lobotomies, which involved slicing and dicing neural connections between millions of neurons. (How did they count that?)

Some 65 years later there are lots of scientists MWTB and they seem to find enough subjects willing to be messed with. ECT is still alive but much changed from the old days (medication, no convulsions, no pain, no broken bones). The latest MWTB is Deep Brain Stimulation, which involves implanting a pair of electrodes in the brain, which are controlled by a generator implanted in the chest. Other related treatments include vagus nerve stimulation and repetitive transcranial magnetic stimulation, and probably others I have not heard of.

For instructive value, I focus here on one development that has gone wrong in some respects: Magnet Therapy. Tallahassee is an appropriate place to focus on magnets given that the FSU magnet is the biggest and most powerful in the world. Google these two words and you get 523,000 hits. Big business? Estimates of sales of magnets annually run up to a billion dollars ($300 million U.S.).

And it should be much bigger if you look at what adherents say it does: relieves pain; moderates depression, cancer, and schizophrenia; removes toxins from the body and increases the flow of oxygen. Nothing was said about washing the dishes. And from Sharper Image, you can get a "Dual-Head Personal Massager with Magnetic Therapy," in a somewhat penis-shaped device that was said to do more than your average vibrator.

You can say goodbye to that expensive vet and keep your dog healthy with any number of magnetic collars, blankets, etc.

Not everyone signed on. The first sentence of an article in the *British Medical Journal*: "We believe there is a worldwide epidemic of useless magnet therapy." And another article with the headline, "Magnet Therapy: A Billion-dollar Boondoggle."

It seems to me that all of these brain stimulations have several things in common.

- The subjects of most of these MWTB studies have been those who were severely impaired and not responsive to other treatments.

- A number of problems limit generalizations: small sample size, participants not randomly assigned to groups.

- When there are positive results, researchers are frequently unable to say what was causative.

This is fascinating research and we are making some progress in understanding how the brain works. The National Institute of Mental Health, along with other agencies, continues to fund projects to that end. Support these efforts, but with a critical eye.

The Ups and Downs of Living with Parkinson's

Michael Kinley's latest book, *Old Age: A Beginners Guide*, was reviewed in *The New York Times* on April 24, 2016. He learned that he had Parkinson's disease in 1993 when he was 43, and for eight years he kept his problems from the public. As his symptoms progressed and became obvious, he outed himself.

As the number of boomers soared to 79 million, he learned that about one in three would have some form of dementia and that Parkinson's can affect cognitive functions. He accurately predicted a flood of books on the subject and worked to get his out before the deluge.

I and my cohort are a generation ahead of him, and well into the old-old category, which brings its own diminishments and losses. Biking, tennis, Interstate driving, are activities no longer safe for me. My ears call for aides. I have lost three or four inches in height by age 88.

Now, back to Parkinson's. In earlier columns, I mentioned a time or two that Mr. Parkinson had befriended me, but did not give any details. It's always with you and it has its own special side effects: loss of smell, drooling, stooped posture, awkward gait, mild cognitive impairment (a label I get in part because when asked to name in 30 seconds animals whose names begin with a "C", after cat, cow, camel, my mind goes completely blank).

The reviewer of Kinsley's book said that Kinsley made a point of saying the book was not about Parkinson's, but in fact, it was the basic thread throughout. You cannot avoid the demands made by Parkinson's but need to work to prevent it becoming all-consuming.

All you can do is play the hand you're dealt. It's not all bad. Lots of people want to help. Expectations are low. You can get away with not wearing a tie. By the time you can get your credit card out of your pocket, someone else has the restaurant bill. Not to worry about coming up with the name of the man approaching you, as he is likely to give it to you: "Hi, I'm Bill Jones, your next door neighbor." A handicapped parking permit is not all that hard to get. When going somewhere with friends they are likely to insist on driving. When exiting a crowded event, most people will let you break line. Your kids are likely to visit more often.

Parkinson's is a movement disorder, and the need to keep active, along with medication, are two recommendations that the experts agree on. There is evidence that it can make a difference in muscle tone, balance, range of motion, and improved psychological outlook. I assume that any exercise might be helpful but situations where the person is forced to a higher intensity over time are most effective. Recent studies with bicycling were convincing enough to prompt me to buy a stationary one. There is a report of a man who cannot walk but rides for miles. Not unlike the many who cannot walk but can run.

If you don't want to check out my bike, you may be interested in one of the following: yoga, tai chi, dance, boxing, Pilates.

Sunday, May 29, 2016

Genes Rule, but We Still Have 'Free Will'

You may want to pay more attention here than usual. While you were out shopping or falling asleep before the TV, I have been working at my computer to show how much the geneticists are taking responsibility for most of our behavior. Note the following facts, all of which have some basis in science.

- Personality traits and happiness are largely inherited.

- There is a genetic link to the ruthlessness of dictators like Hitler.

- The age of loss of virginity is dependent upon a variety of factors, including genes, which account for 25 percent of the total.

- Genes account for about 1/2 of the variance in the development of loneliness.

- There seems to be a genetic contribution to certain addictions, including sex and gambling.

- Some cultures are hardwired for a vegetarian diet. Cultures from Africa and Asia have eaten a vegetarian diet for so long that if they stray from the diet they are subject to a higher risk of a number of serious health problems.

- Whether you prefer to get up at the crack of dawn or work late into the night is probably linked with genes connected to the circadian rhythm. (Morning people are happier than Night Owls. Quality of sleep is more important than quantity.) There are people who are energized on four hours of sleep ("short-sleepers"), believed to have genetic mutations on the hDAC2 gene that runs in the family.

- A recent study in the *Journal of Personality* focused on 800 pairs of fraternal and identical twins, concluded that success is genetically determined. Yes, there can be problems in defining "success."

- The elderly are concerned about falling and breaking bones. Researchers have identified a genetic mutation that regulates bone density, giving some people extremely dense bones that are practically unbreakable.

- What we eat can influence cholesterol but genetics play a big role. Mutations result in a deficiency of a particular protein linked with having higher levels of "good" cholesterol.

- There are at least six genes associated with how your body processes caffeine. Some influence the rewarding effects of caffeine that make you want more. Some are linked to how the body metabolizes caffeine. Others explain why in some cases, caffeine does not interfere with sleep.

- If your cheeks go rosy after one glass of wine you may have a mutation that interferes with the ability of a liver enzyme to convert the alcohol into acetate.

- And finally, for what it is worth, in the bird world there are "cross-dressers" that appear to be genetically driven. There are male birds that can simulate the coloring, etc., of females, in order to get close to them.

Knowing what you know now, in some circles, bad behavior on your part might be excused with, "My genes made me do it." But this will not get you far. However strong the genetic effect, it is subject to modification through psychological and environmental interference. There is still room for some "free will."

I close with my repeated injunction to keep in mind that what we know today may not hold tomorrow. It was Walter Cronkite who said, "We must be ever skeptical but not become cynical. Cynicism deadens an approach a journalist should properly have toward a story."

Sunday, August 14, 2016

Reflections on Life as Summer Draws to an End

In a matter of weeks, we have attended the college graduation of a grandson in California; the wedding of a granddaughter in Pennsylvania; and the funeral of a brother in Virginia. Lots of back and forth across the country, with some of the family making it for all three events. Lots of laughter and tears. Lots to reflect on once we were back home. Here is a sample of thoughts that floated to the top.

Life changes and moves on. The presence of three great-grandchildren, eight grandchildren (one of them pregnant) and their significant others, would have pleased my mother. Her six grandchildren were girls and she was anxious that there might not be enough males to carry on the Miller genes. Not to worry, Mom.

There would be much to make her uncomfortable, including good people moving in together without being married and sometimes having a child. The debate about LGBT would have evoked a blush if you told her what the letters stood for.

The high point of the wedding was the dancing. A "high energy" band played for hours and the dance floor was crowded with an age spread from 1 to 90. My 4-year-old great-granddaughter cried when pulled from the floor late in the evening. No particular skill was needed, just shake whatever you could, once in a while thrusting a fist up and giving a yelp.

The high point of the college graduation was the ending of the reading of the names of the 400 plus graduates. There must be a better way that would satisfy both students and parents, but I can't think what it would be.

Now for my brother Bill. His last months were not good, following a pattern familiar to most of us. Increasing number of falls, some dementia (good days and bad), wandering, severe memory loss, and a loss of the personality that made him who he was. His wife and their three daughters struggled valiantly to keep him at home until his death at 93.

We think we know one another, but often there are dimensions not obvious to us, things that surprise. Things not declared for reasons unknown. Unknown to family were Bill's two medals from World War II. More interesting to me was a poem, "A Prayer of Thanksgiving" by Elizabeth, Countess of Craven, England (1750-1828), which he carried in his wallet for years. On the back were his birthday and the birthday of his wife. I knew he was a man of faith but I never thought of him as both a sentimentalist and a romantic. If someone had told me about this poem I would have said, "Wrong wallet."

From June 8 through July 19 we traveled about 8,000 miles. I was aware that I was doing some things for the last time, as might be expected for someone in their late 80s. Probably there were lots of people in California and Newport News that I would not see again. All of us are at risk for an unending list of last times. The trick is to focus on what remains, find the fun, pay attention, review your priorities. Remember the past and face the future.

Interesting Times for Young and Old Alike

You have to admit we are living in interesting times. The world scene may not have changed much, with most of our energy devoted to trying to kill one another. But at the local and national level, there are developments worth talking about.

The old-timers (OTs), us, are the fastest growing age segment and we have to get serious in thinking about how we are to deal with this. At the other end of the spectrum, we have the millennials, now outnumbering the baby boomers, and much in the news. They sharpened their teeth on the campaign of Bernie Sanders but seem to have gotten over his loss. Let us hope that they continue to be interested in the political process and the fate of our country.

I recently read about a survey (sorry, can't find the source) finding that millennials preferred being online over real-life sex. Beat out by a phone? If this is accurate, we may be in real trouble. Maybe this is the time to plan for interventions for electronic addicts. On the other hand, we should never take one survey as gospel.

Along the way, there are some interesting if unimportant, developments that merit attention. Note the following samples.

Shaved heads. Research reveals that having a shaved head conveys an appearance of being tougher and more powerful than others. It indicates influence and authority, increasing the strength perception of a man 13 percent. All of this backed by experiments conducted by Albert Mannes, a lecturer at Wharton School of Business. Silly me, when I first saw shaved heads I thought there was a problem with lice, medical treatment, or a religious requirement. Did the governor of Florida know something we didn't? As he gets closer to Trump might he persuade the man to shave his head?

Style. The *Tallahassee Democrat* recently ran a story on actor Zachary Quinto, with pictures of him in an array of the latest in men's clothing. The caption was "Look good and prosper," subjects I would normally take a pass on. But the pictures caught my eye. It looked as if the clothes had been sewed on, particularly the pants. I don't understand how a man could tolerate such tightness in an especially sensitive area of the body, not to mention the possibility of a rise in voice register. Any pockets would be useless because there is no way a hand could overcome that tightness. I have to believe Quinto wore them only long enough to have the pictures taken. Never mind, the OTs have only a passing interest in this. Our emphasis is on remembering the rule not to leave the house wearing a T-shirt that has no collar and to wash clothes frequently.

Pain. Most of our older friends spend a lot of time trying to control pain. For appearances, a few will wear shoes or other clothing that is mildly pain-inducing. I still don't understand the young that pay to have a ring inserted in the nose, lip, ear, whatever. Or undergo the pain that comes with tattoos, along with the possibility of infection. Or undergo surgery to improve what most of us think is an OK appearance.

But we can appreciate the pain endured in training for the beauty we saw in the just completed Olympics. And the morning paper has a nice story out of Rio. During the women's 5,000 meters, a runner fell

Robert Miller (Kent's father) with great-granddaughter Christina Riccardi at Lake Ella, Tallahassee, 1984 (left); Kent with great-granddaughter Katherine Johnson (Christina Riccardi's daughter) at Lake Ella, Tallahassee, 2016 (Right)

and another runner, a complete stranger, dropped out of the race to help her up.

Much of what I have mentioned above is rather fluffy stuff. But we can't deny that underneath it there are some serious issues that demand attention. Change is the one thing we can count on, and we should be out there trying to help shape it.

Youth is generally optimistic, energetic, inventive. Most young people are trying to find their own way plus new ways to live. They embrace both fads and some enduring truths. One of them is that generation to generation we need each other's help. In all the flow and flux there is a thread of continuity reflected in the attached pictures. The first picture is my father walking around Lake Ella with his great-granddaughter Christina. (A *Democrat* photographer took the picture in 1983 or 1984.) The other picture has me walking around Lake Ella with great-granddaughter Katherine (Christina's daughter).

Friday, September 23, 2016

Does Trump Show Signs of Being a Clinical Narcissist?

While at a rented beach house, morning coffee in hand, I noted an object I could not identify. An attached tag read, "Self-portrait stick which allows you to focus on yourself."

When I was an adolescent if somebody displayed an excessive attention to self, they were said to be showboating, hot-dogging it. The football player who had caught a pass for a touchdown might point to the quarterback who had thrown the ball or raise a hand to the applauding crowd. Anything more would not have been cool.

That was yesterday. Today you might see backslapping, chest bumps, prancing, negative gestures for the opposing team. When these behaviors are carried to an extreme, the shrinks get involved.

The American Association of Psychiatry's *Diagnostic and Statistical Manual of Mental Disorders* contains the following: "Narcissistic personality disorder is a mental disorder in which people have an inflated sense of their own importance, a deep need for admiration and a lack of empathy for others. But behind this mask of ultra-confidence lies a fragile self-esteem that's vulnerable to the slightest criticism."

There are several scales to measure the degree of narcissism, most of them taking into account some version of these characteristics. A diagnosis of Narcissistic Personality Disorder may be made when five or more of these items are present.

1 Grandiose sense of self-importance.

2 Preoccupation with fantasies of unlimited success.

3 Belief that he/she is special and unique.

4 Has a sense of entitlement.

5 Often envious of others and believes others are envious of him/her.

6 Interpersonally exploitative.

7 Lacks empathy.

8 Shows arrogant behavior or attitudes.

9 Requires excessive admiration.

Some have suggested that Donald Trump meets these criteria. I leave this decision up to you, by letting him speak for himself.

- "The beauty of me is that I am very rich."

- "All of the women on 'The Apprentice' flirt with me – consciously or unconsciously. That is to be expected."

- "Women find his power almost as much of a turn-on as his money," (referring to himself).

- "A person who is very flat chested is very hard to be a 10."

- "My fingers are as long and beautiful, as, it has been well documented, are various other parts of my body."

- "I will build a great wall – and nobody builds walls better than me and I will make Mexicans pay for that wall."

- "My whole life is about winning. I don't lose often."

- "If Hillary Clinton can't satisfy her husband what makes you think she can satisfy America."

- "My I.Q. is one of the highest – and you all know it! Please don't feel so stupid or insecure, it's not your fault."

Having read these statements, what kind of grade would you give Trump? Can you see him as President, negotiating a peace agreement with world leaders?

Famous Last Words

My grandfather was the champion wrestler in his county and a Lutheran minister. To an 8-year-old, he was a formidable figure.

I was taken in to see him on his deathbed, and as we entered the room, we heard a string of curses obviously coming from him and I was quickly whisked out of the room. This is a vague memory for me. I can't be sure of all the facts.

Thinking about dying this week, I remembered this incident and wondered about other people's last words. I went online and found much information on this topic. There are famous people there along with death-row inmates.

We turn to last words as if they reflect the essence of the person, a key to the personality, a measure of what the person considers important. Certainly, there is something to that, but they should be taken primarily as a source of entertainment.

Here are a few to whet your appetite.

W. C. Fields sounded a little angry: "God damn the whole friggin' world and everyone in it but you, Carloto." (His mistress).

So did Eugene O'Neill: "I know it. I know it. Born in a hotel room and God damn it, I died in a hotel room."

John Spenkelink on death row: "Capital punishment means those without capital get the punishment."

Death row inmate Thomas Grasso: speaking of his last meal, "I did not get my Spaghetti-O's. I got spaghetti. I want the press to know."

The biggest surprise to me was how many last words are focused on being funny.

A man named Appel, about to be executed said, "You are about to see a fried apple." Likewise, a man named French asked, "How about this for a headline? French fried."

When the Comtesse de Vermicellis farted as she was dying, she said, "Good. A woman who can fart is not dead."

A man being moved to the gallows pointed to the trap door and asked if they were sure it was safe.

When Groucho Marx was dying he quipped, "This is no way to live."

As drummer Buddy Rich was being prepared for surgery, he was asked if there was anything he could not take. He replied, "country music."

When TV announcer Charles Gussman was dying, he removed his oxygen mask and said, "And now for a final word from our sponsor."

"You be good. See you tomorrow. I love you." The last words of Alex, an African grey parrot used in psychology research at Brandeis. He was found dead in his cage the next day. This was his sign-off every night.

These few quotes provided amusement for me. Thousands more await you at Wikiquote Last words, alphabetized by last name.

The internet really is a wonderful thing.

With Many People Lonely, RentAfriend Has Merits

A recent issue of *The Week* contained an article detailing how to rent-a-friend in Tokyo. You start by becoming a member of Client Partners, an agency with eight branches across the country. The bulk of the clients just want basic, uncomplicated companionship: e.g., somebody to talk about aging parents; a male to attend activities of children who do not have a man in the house; a stand-in for the sister of the bride, who was not able to make it to the ceremony; someone to accompany for dinner and a show.

Client Partners provides access to the profiles of people who can be hired by the hour to provide emotional contact with a friendly person and help with specific problems. It is a rapidly expanding phenomena and seems a good fit for the current culture of Japan. Single parents are heavy users of the agency.

I was not familiar with the booming rent-a-friend industry and wondered if the U.S. was a player. Indeed, it is. (Several networks had recently carried stories about it, missed by me.)

RentAFriend.com allows you to contact friends from all over the world. (Membership as of Oct. 8, 2016, was 621,585.) The clientele seems to be the same as in Japan: companionship for a meal, movie, to learn a skill, for guidance in a new city, for attendance at a sports event, whatever. No sex and no borrowing money. RentAFriend makes clear that it is not a dating website or escort agency, and services are strictly for friendship.

You start by paying a $25 monthly fee ($79 yearly). Then you post a profile of yourself along with a picture. Friends charge from $20 and up to $50 or more an hour, often negotiable. You visit the site, review profiles, and make contact through the website. There are no restrictions and both parties know that the relationship may end after the first meeting.

In my reading, I did not find any reference to older people but it seems to me that it could be a great service. Many seniors have lost a mate, may not be driving, and if there are family members, may be concerned about "being a burden." Currently, as I understand it, there is no vetting of friends and some may be needed to protect vulnerable seniors. This potential problem is not mentioned on the website.

RentAFriend lists over a hundred members in Tallahassee and from the profiles I saw, it is much like a place to meet potential dates. A great majority are in their 20s and would have no interest in befriending old people. To be of help to older members, there would have to be a dramatic change in the number and variety of profiles.

The need for friendship is reflected in a recent survey that found that one in four U.S. adults are lonely.

When at age 82 my father came down from Virginia to live with us, we were busy and he certainly experienced loneliness. Eventually, he found a group of older men that met daily for coffee. It would have been great to have had RentAFriend to provide companionship, take him to a baseball game, etc. Maybe someone will pick up the challenge.

Good Kind of Pride Is Driving Force in Success

Why did Paul Gauguin abandon middle-class life to follow the path of the starving artist? What explains the massive success of Steve Jobs, a man with great ideas but weak programming skills and a questionable managerial style? How did Dean Karnazes, the famed "Ultramarathon Man", transform himself from a directionless desk jockey into an extreme athlete who once ran 50 marathons in 50 days?

These are the questions that psychologist Jessica Tracy, at the University of British Columbia, examines in her book *Take Pride, Why the Deadliest Sin Holds the Secret to Human Success*, published in the fall of 2016. She argues that yes, there is a dark side to pride as one of the worst of the seven deadly sins, but pride also pushes us to be our best. Research has shown that it "boosts creativity, motivates altruism, and confers power and prestige on those who display it."

The point is that there are two kinds of pride: Authentic and Hubristic.

Authentic pride is based on a realistic appraisal of one's competencies, abilities, and achievements; we typically feel it when we have worked hard for an achievement and it has been acknowledged. This generates feelings of confidence and tends to make us more productive, creative, empathic.

Hubristic pride, on the other hand, is mostly not based in reality, instead manifests itself as a grandiose, inflated sense of self. It is egoistic, arrogant, conceited, not particularly conscientious, often disagreeable, has problematic relationships, is aggressive and unempathetic. (Donald Trump admirers will not like this book, as Tracy uses him as the perfect example of hubristic pride.)

We should be grateful to Tracy for making the point that there are two kinds of pride, with one of them to be celebrated.

For several years, her research has been focused on some aspect of pride, finding characteristics that seem to be universal, cutting across cultures, e.g., experiencing pride evokes "a happy smile," unique posture, head tilted back, chest puffed out, hands on hips or raised in the air. Tracy found this identical pattern in women and men, and people born blind, suggesting something very basic was going on.

She claims that pride can even override pleasure as a motivating force and that many notable achievements and inventions throughout history can be traced back to it. She would likely feel that pride was the ruling force for the people mentioned in the first paragraph above.

Tracy worries about a recent epidemic of lying and cheating, such as Lance Armstrong's illegal doping, social psychologist Dietrich Stapel's fabrication of data, etc. She sees these events as stemming from a hubristic pride.

Now, back to the two basic prides. As with most things, they are fluid, and at times we may slide back and forth to some extent. You do not need to be a psychologist to know that having the qualities listed under the "good" pride will stand you in good stead.

Hold on to the pride.

(I have not read this book but have read other writing by Tracy on the same subject. She is widely recognized for her research.)

Think About It: Evidence Points to Exercise Gains

The word is that there has been a drop in dementia rates due in part to better treatment, changes in the age structure of the population and some related stuff I can't recall, but if you are old or hope to be, you or somebody you love is likely to experience significant cognitive loss.

Don't look to those puzzles and games created to challenge the brain. Unfortunately, there is no scientific evidence to support their claims. At one point things got so bad that the Federal Trade Commission issued a warning of fraudulent claims.

Don't expect a lot from medication aside from a buffering of symptoms (exception: drugs such as dopamine for Parkinson's). There is a possibility of help from some of the memory assistance drugs.

There is one thing where the evidence is strong. Exercise. It goes to the top of the list. There is a steady stream of affirming research reports similar to the two I report here.

Walking 200 minutes per week on average at age 70 has been shown to not only maintain cognitive function, but it also results in an increase in the size of certain parts of the brain.

Another striking finding came out of the University of Maryland School of Public Health. Physically fit adults ages 50-80 had a 10-day period when they stopped all exercise. MRI brain imaging showed a significant decrease in blood flow to several brain regions.

A number of our friends regularly go to gyms and some have personal trainers. A local church just announced that they were adding two additional buildings on its grounds, both community centers (gyms?). The word about exercise is out. People just have to get with it. (Not everybody buys in. One of my docs said three times a week is plenty. My physical therapist pulled me aside, saying that daily would be good.)

Recent research has added to our understanding of brain function. The brain is much more plastic than we thought, constantly enlarging and narrowing. Scientists at the University of Utah found that engaging in prayer has the same effect on religious people's brain as having sex.

Now, back to larger issues, much of which will sound familiar. Not much new here. My advice is to guard against the tendency to fold up the tent. Get out of the house. If you like work, carry on with what you can. Engage in activities that challenge your brain. Keep a note on the bathroom mirror: use it or lose it. You will find lots of people eager to do everything for you – tying shoelaces, cutting toenails (short line for this one); getting out of a chair. Don't give in. Do as much for yourself as you can.

My second piece of advice is to make sure you have in writing what you want or do not want as things close down, and talk about it with those who will be making decisions.

And finally, it is OK to ignore all the stuff above and say to the hell with it, I'm tired. The ball is in your court.

Pessimism vs. Optimism: Which Way Do You Lean?

Pessimism. A tendency to take the gloomiest possible view of a situation.

Optimism. A tendency or disposition to expect the best possible outcome or to dwell upon the most hopeful aspects of a situation.

Which camp are you in? Do you care? Does it matter? Can you move from one position to another? Psychologists and others have tried for decades to answer these questions.

At first skimming through the data, the pessimists would likely be scrambling to transfer membership. Look at this sample of findings: 10-year study revealed that optimists had lived 8-10 years longer; had greater overall health, more vitality, less pain, greater mobility; employers look to hire optimistic workers; Harvard students who were optimistic at age 25 were healthier at 45 and 60; optimistic sports teams performed better than the pessimistic.

A recent 11-year study of 2,267 middle-aged and older men and women found that pessimists were more than twice as likely to have died from heart disease. The lead author said, "Your personality traits can make physical health worse." It is not known what causes the association but some speculate that pessimism may increase inflammation, and may prevent people from searching for healthy habits.

(If you are curious about where you stand, you can easily learn by searching the internet for optimism scales, which consist of a limited number of questions. If you have nothing better to do, you might take several scales to check consistency.)

The transition from pessimism to optimism may not be easy, but the authors assure us that it can be done. A study of 500 paired identical twins revealed that genes contribute to about 25 percent of the ultimate choice. That leaves plenty of room to change should you choose to do so. A 12-week study of depressed patients found that cognitive therapy was more helpful than medications.

Points to keep in mind:

Most of us are spread across a continuum, not at the extremes.

The Presidential election may have turned many liberals into pessimists, convinced that the new administration is set on destroying our democracy. (A real optimist sees goodness in the fact that things are going to change, and knows that this too will pass.)

Some observers believe that the more we try to be happy by thinking positively, the unhappier we make ourselves.

British journalist Oliver Burkeman thinks this is true and makes the case in his book *The Antidote: Happiness for People Who Can't Stand Positive Thinking*. He suggests five actions:

- Accept your thoughts for what they are.

- Focus on the present moment. Don't judge whether they are good or bad.

- Learn from "failure."

- Stamp out your need for self-esteem.

- Allow yourself to think about mortality. "By not being afraid of death, you also won't be afraid of the future and therefore better able to accept the present."

So, we have here two radically different approaches in the search for fulfillment. You might say optimism versus realism. You should have no trouble taking from both. If you are coming down the stretch, you should have quit worrying about your failures. Continue to be helpful if you are able. Talk freely about death. Look for laughter.

Talking to Self May Engage the Brain

In 1954, I was an intern at the Houston VA Hospital. At that time, it was not unusual to see patients muttering and talking loudly to themselves. This was interpreted as a symptom of a serious mental disease.

Fast forward some 60 years and on any day you could likely hear this exchange in our house: "Did you call me?" "No. I was talking to myself." Only recently have we learned that was a wise thing to do. Should you be listening quietly to your thoughts or saying things out loud?

Experts tell us that paying attention to what we are thinking or talking out loud helps to organize thinking, screens out distractions, improves memory, reinforces the message, and a lot more. Betty must have known this intuitively for she has me read the grocery list out loud. Last week I picked up the wrong list, but at the store, I recalled 11 out of 14 items. (If you knew the quality of my memory you might think this a miracle.)

Charles Fernyhough, a British psychologist, has a new book titled *The Voices Within: The History and Science Of How We Talk To Ourselves.* Fernyhough writes out of his 27 years of research on the topic and I found the going a little difficult at times. (You can skip the 41 pages of footnotes.)

But there are examples of readily understood research such as the following: Take two groups in a dart throwing contest, instructing one to think positively (I can do this), and the other to think negatively (I can't do this). Those who thought positively consistently earned higher scores. In an experiment, 20 people were given the name of an object to find in a grocery store while bound to silence. In a second trial, they repeated the search while saying the name of the object, which made for a quicker find.

Not everyone hears voices or talks much to themselves, either covertly (silent) or overtly (out loud). For those who do, a large majority spend 20 percent to 25 percent of their waking time doing so. Certain groups have higher numbers, e.g., fiction writers, including Fernyhough.

Throughout history, the religiously oriented have heard God speak to them. Increasing interest is reflected in a new international organization, the Hearing Voices Movement.

It should be clear that the references here do not apply to the truly broken and mentally ill who have heard a voice instructing them to kill certain people.

Social scientists are working hard to bring more science to the attempt to understand how we talk to ourselves. Researchers are using fMRI to observe inner speech, and Cognitive Behavioral Treatment as a means of controlling inner thoughts. There is a lot to be learned, but an increasing number of tools to help.

At one point in writing this column, I was not satisfied with what I had written and dropped it. Later, I assumed a more positive mood, saying out loud "Miller, you have written hundreds of columns and you can finish this one."

March 5, 2017

Libraries Stay Relevant for Old and Young

Several years ago, there was a lot of hand-wringing in Britain about the demise of the public library. Three hundred and forty-three libraries closed, with many more expected to join them soon. Cuts in budgets, hours, and programs. Some observers saw the problems spreading across the western world and the death of the public library.

Wayne Wiegand, author of the recent *Our Lives: A People's History of the American Public Library* tells us to relax, Americans love their public library. The Pew Research Center found that in the previous decade every major institution (government, churches, banks) fell in esteem, except the public library.

The Institute of Museum and Library Sciences notes that 55 percent of new Americans use a library at least once a week. A Massachusetts librarian explained, "We have huge resources for newcomers to the country... for legal resources, testing preparations, help with homework."

The U.S. has at least 18,000 public libraries, more than ever. (More than the number of McDonald's.) Why do we love them? Wiegand tells us in three broad categories: 1. making useful information accessible, 2. providing space to help construct community, 3. the transformative potential that reading, viewing and listening to the commonplace stories that public libraries provide in a variety of forms (books, films, DVDs, etc.).

From the start, public librarians have been helpful with social justice issues. An excellent example is racial segregation. In the 1930s the Atlanta library welcomed blacks. Maya Angelou had this to say: "I always knew from that moment, from the time I found myself at home in that little segregated library in the South, all the way up until I walked up the steps of the New York City Library, I always felt, in any town, if I can get to a library, I'll be okay. It really helped me as a child, and that never left me. So I have a special place for every library, in my heart of hearts."

To see how we are faring in Tallahassee, I caught up with Cay Hohmeister, Director of Leon County LeRoy Collins Libraries (main and six branches scattered around town). She conveyed confidence that things are moving along smoothly, although, in response to a question, she acknowledged that additional funding would permit an expansion of services.

The lending of books and related materials is still a strong function (1.8 million checkouts last year). Beyond that, there is a lot going on at the LeRoy Collins Library, surely some things that may surprise you.

You will find displays of the work of local artists. Conference rooms are available for various community organizations. There is an area for computers, printers, etc. for the public. You can call and get an appointment with a "tech" to help you with your phone or tablet.

There are activities for all ages (book clubs, discussion groups, preschool story hours).

You can conduct job searches. Register to vote. Visit the Consumer Research Center before making a purchase.

There is a lot more, all of it free.

Cay Hohmeister and staff should feel good about what they have created. They get considerable help from volunteers.

The service is tops, as illustrated by my last visit when I went in to pick up a book that was on hold. As it was handed to me I asked if she would search the catalog for another book I wanted. No problem, yes, it is in the stacks on the second floor. Would you like for someone to bring it down? Just have a seat over there. (If I had asked them to shine my shoes, I think they would have found a way to make it happen.)

Now, I know that I look like I need help, but it seems librarians have an almost pathological desire to help others. (What a nice disorder.) My wife tells me that part of a librarian's training is the idea of service and viewing themselves as educators.

(Full transparency requires me to note that three members of my family are librarians.)

Quest to Understand Ourselves Is Lifelong

Most of us are inclined to be interested in learning about ourselves, who we are, particularly in comparison with others.

There is a website containing a 12-minute version of the famous Myers-Briggs personality test. The claim is made that 50 million people have taken the free abbreviated test and for $33 you can receive a premium analysis of your personality. The Myers-Briggs was made in 1945 by two people with limited training and is said to be still in use by government agencies and individuals. Many of you reading this have taken the test.

There is no harm in this if you use it for entertainment. Don't take it seriously, keep in mind the absence of reliability, validity, or anything scientific.

Reading about the Myers-Briggs prompted me to wonder what we have learned about personality traits. Besides, I wouldn't mind learning something about myself. Most of the research has been focused on five personality traits: conscientiousness, agreeableness, neuroticism, openness, extraversion. Others work with four basic types: Envious, Trusting, Optimistic, Pessimistic.

Herewith a sample of studies of some interest:

- Researchers at the University of California, Berkeley, examined data from 132,515 people, ages 21-60. They found that the long-held notion that personality was set early was wrong, as conscientiousness and agreeableness grew in the 30s and continued well into the 60s. These findings held across gender. Openness showed small declines in men and women over time, possibly due to less interest in establishing new relationships than in spending time with family and old friends.

- A psychiatrist at the University of Western Australia said that personality changes in old age are usually minimal, and any significant change is likely caused by changes in the frontotemporal areas of the brain and warrants a neuropsychiatric exam.

- A thousand young people kept a diary of what they ate. Participants who scored higher than average for openness ate more fruit and veggies, and less bad foods. Adventurous people might be healthier than the rest of us. Extroversion also had a positive effect, just not as much as openness.

- In 1950, 1,200 14-year-old students were evaluated in terms of personalities. In 2012, 174 of the original were found and reevaluated. They found no correlation with who they were at 14. "Personality changes only slowly throughout life but by older age, it might be quite different from personality in childhood."

Did I learn anything about myself from this bit of research? Probably not. But it reinforced some beliefs. Even in this time of shrinkage, "last times," the inability to come up with the name of that pear-shaped green fruit that sells for $1.50, a body that refuses commands, fingers that can't button a shirt, sensory loss, mild cognitive impairment, being invisible in certain gatherings, saying goodbye to friends of 50 years. Even at this stage, there is room for change, for love and being loved, for ice cream.

Staycation Brings Lots of Gin Rummy, a Few Surprises

This year, for a variety of reasons, we were unable to take an out-of-town vacation. Betty took this as a challenge to find something that would be a satisfying substitute and came up with the Staycation: a period in which an individual or family stays home and participates in leisure activities within driving distance (Wikipedia). Staycation was popular in 2007-2010, during the financial crisis.

Without knowing much more than that, we decided to give it a two-week shot and went to work on ground rules.

For starters, we planned to sharply limit cooking. Phones would not be answered before noon. No yard work. Mail to go to a box unread. No wasting time traveling to the gym. No one invited to the house. No house maintenance work. Money matters put aside (no balancing the checking book, etc.).

Nap after lunch. Gin rummy and coffee in the afternoon. Network news recorded so we could eliminate commercials. Accept invitations to dinner if someone gets through to us. Go to fixed evening happenings as we liked (e.g., Betty's book clubs and card games). No packing.

We had fun listing the negatives that are frequently a part of vacations. A feeling that you have to go see "X" because you may not come this way again. No standing in line for tickets to events you could miss without hurting. If you are traveling with relatives or friends there will be much time devoted to agreeing where and when to eat. The hotel beds and pillows are not likely to be just right. No shaving or much concern about dress.

The books we wanted to read were there at hand. Both of us had projects that we wanted to complete. Let the good times roll. All this and a chance to get to know each other better. (After 67 years of marriage, Betty still surprises me.)

Things didn't go as planned. The first two days were fine, settling in. The third day I asked Betty how would she feel if I made a cheese omelet, bacon, muffins. She said she thought she could handle that. Two days later both of us were less than eager to go out for dinner. We found good reasons for calling the children in the morning. We fixed sandwiches to take to a lake where we could feed the ducks. It was so hot the ducks were not interested and we beat it back to the air conditioning.

We decided to open the mail, 95 percent solicitations. A little progress was made on our projects, but we are close to not needing projects. There was nothing wrong with the Staycation, and we will be taking more of them as traveling gets more difficult.

We take our almost daily game of gin seriously, and after all these years Betty has only a 6-game lead.

We're back online. With the *Tallahassee Democrat* and the *NYT*, there is enough to get the juices flowing in the mornings and get all those petitions signed.

Many Reasons to Grieve, Many Ways to Cope

Many of us have been down the grieving road, probably more than once. Maybe not for someone close, but enough to know it's bumpy, hard to get off. There are many reasons to grieve, perhaps with death the most common.

Several factors shape our response to a death including age, the degree of closeness, whether the person was in pain and wanted off the hook and quality of life.

Keep in mind that there are no rules for grieving, no "correct" way of doing it. What works for one person could well mean disaster for the next. But in recent years we have learned some things that have been helpful to a number of people (e.g., talking about your condition, keeping a journal, knowing that it is normal for moods to swing from day to day).

Recent access to surveys by the census means I don't have to make up the numbers as we try to get a fix on how things go for elderly people who have lost a spouse. Here are a few things recently learned:

About 40 percent of women who are 65 or older are widowed, and the corresponding figure for men is 13 percent. Sifting through the research, the following conclusions have some merit.

- Grief is not forever. George Bonanno, a psychologist at Columbia University, found that the core symptoms of grief—anxiety, depression, shock, intrusive thoughts—had lifted by six months for 50 percent of the bereaved.

- Counseling is not necessary for healing.

- Humor can lighten the load.

- Drawing on happy memories of the deceased can help.

But grief comes in all shapes to all ages.

Sheryl Sandberg, chief operating officer at Facebook, and author of the best-selling book *Lean In*, had been married 11 years when she and her husband Dave were vacationing in Mexico, their two children back home. She had been by the pool napping, and upon waking, realized that Dave had been gone for some time. Racing to the gym, where he had planned to go, she found him on the floor next to an elliptical trainer, his head in a pool of blood. The death was totally unexpected.

An autopsy, a spokesperson for Sandberg's Foundation said, showed that he died of coronary heart disease and that he had a cardiac arrhythmia.

Sometime later Sandberg and Adam Grant, a psychologist, co-authored a book just published, *Option B: Facing Adversity, Building Resilience, and Finding Joy.* She writes in detail about the initial shock and grief, on through how individuals can override the bad stuff. Many of her points are backed by references assembled by Grant (30 pages of endnotes). Some critics say, "Not much new here." But certainly, some readers will be interested and find hope in it.

There are a lot of people out there eager to educate us on how to grieve. Some of it is helpful. If you want to go back to work or volunteering three days after your loss, do it. (Sandberg took 10 days.) Listen to family and friends. The National Institute on Aging can provide some helpful advice, starting with the article "Mourning the Death of a Spouse."

As we age I am acutely aware that we deal almost daily with loss. For example, we don't see or hear as well as we did. We need more help, sometimes having to leave a place we lived in for years. Because I see this all around, I am even more impressed with how adaptable we are, how we come to terms with our daily griefs and still find meaning and pleasure in life.

Sunday, August 13, 2017

Being 90:
It's Ok to Play the
Old Card Now

Our children gave me a party for my 90th birthday. Never mind that my birthday is in November. The children are scattered across the country and the thought was that travel would be easier in the summer. (Looking at me, they might have thought it best not to gamble on my being here in November.) They came and we had a great party with about 20 at meal time. Conversation was fun, lots of laughter. Several people asked in different ways what I had learned in 90 years. I have no memory of what I said, but here are a few thoughts for those on the road to becoming seniors. Not in order of significance.

- Don't be reluctant to play the old card. When I make contact with someone, I explain, "I'm 90 and I have a mild cognitive impairment and hope you will be patient." Works to my benefit every time (except the few occasions when I have someone who hates their grandparents).

- Get rid of the drawer full of "work clothes", you probably will not be doing any heavy work.

- At 90, wearing your shirt out looks a bit silly, but what the hell, if you like the look, go for it.

- Avoid mirrors. The only time you need one is to place the bandage where you cut your face.

- If you live with another, avoid telling the same story for the nth time. Get an agreement such as Betty and I have. Say to the guilty partner, "When was that?" which serves as a reminder that this is an old tale.

- I am about to violate the suggestion above (Betty is out). Yes, I have a thing about neckties and many of you have heard it. But it is important. I can name a number of public figures that I believe have been wearing the tie too tightly, cutting off oxygen to the brain. Do you have a better reason for their behavior?

- But we are winning this one. Catch the absence of ties on the evening news and I can report my ties are gone. Except one. My son-in-law has given me a tie that slips over the head, has a nice Windsor knot, can be adjusted with a simple pull, and looks like the real thing. I hope to have it cremated along with my body.

- Try not to get annoyed by the hard of hearing. Many of them wear hearing aids but still can't hear everything. It is not their fault but their loss. This failure to communicate is one of the most isolating things in old age.

- Check zippers periodically.

- You don't need to untie a shoelace to get attention. Laces become untied by themselves. People, even strangers, like to say, "Let me tie that shoelace. Wouldn't want you to trip." You will help by making someone feel good, and they will help you by keeping you upright.

- Don't be offended when someone pats you on the leg or shoulder. They would be surprised if you took it as any more than a friendly gesture. And you should take it as such.

- One other thing. Regardless of how strong and loving the bond with your children, be sensitive to what you ask of them. They have activities and demands stemming from their children and grandchildren.

Enough. Time for a nap.

Columnist Kent Miller Left His Mark in the Democrat and in the Community

Nada Hassanein, *Democrat staff writer*

Following a playful and honest column about being 90 years old, *Tallahassee Democrat* columnist Kent Miller passed away Sunday night.

For the past three years as a *Democrat* columnist, Miller was known for his editorials about aging and reflections about topics the elderly grapple with — from maintaining relationships in old age to memory loss to navigating the healthcare system — and life in between.

But he also wrote about the intangible concepts with which everyone contends: the unseen world of emotions. Love, worry, happiness — all of it.

A retired Florida State University professor of psychology, Miller also ran a mental health center. Harnessing his knowledge of the human psyche, coupled with wisdom, his columns appealed to not just the aging, but also the introspective, the curious.

In his column "Being 90: It's OK to play the old card now," which ran Sunday, he gave his two cents about being an octogenarian. "Check zippers periodically," he advised, and, "At 90, wearing your shirt out looks a bit silly, but what the hell, if you like the look, go for it."

He'd likely be the first to do that himself. The bearded, emeritus professor loathed wearing a tie, his daughter Jill Theg said. He didn't care about those "external trappings."

But he did have one favorite accessory — perhaps the one he was never begrudged about wearing: a gold-plated Girard Perregaux watch gifted to him by his wife on their first anniversary 66 years ago. He wore it the day he died.

Despite the serious issues he tackled professionally and in his columns, with a twinkle in his eye he often turned a tedious situation into a game. He'd coax Theg and her siblings out of boredom during long car rides with a quick-witted, "OK, how many red cars do you think will cross this intersection in the next 10 minutes?" He'd entertain his grandchildren by seeing how long he could walk with a teacup on his head before it fell.

As a girl, Theg and her father would sit in the living room together on mellow nights for impromptu duets. She'd sing "I Can't Give You Anything But Love" and he'd strum his guitar.

Theg remembers many people knocking on their front door asking for a few minutes with her dad.

"He was a person people turned to all his life for his wisdom and insight," she said. A clinical psychologist by trade and a listener by nature, in conversations his gaze seldom flinched. "He made you feel like you were the center of the universe."

While mild-mannered, Miller was a provocateur, with a longtime history of publicly calling out injustices.

"He had very strong opinions, but he was not pushy about them — he was very respectful of other people's opinions," said Greg Riccardi, Miller's son-in-law. "He had a very strong sense of social justice: civil liberties, a right to health care, protection of the earth. All of those things were very important to him."

"I am unbelievably lucky to have a father-in-law like that," he added.

Miller wrote about the involuntary detainment of the mentally ill in his *Managing Madness: The Case against Civil Commitment* and a book opposing the death penalty called *To Kill and Be Killed* that he co-authored with his wife.

A man of high energy and high spirits, he balanced his research and writing with running, keeping a jingling set of keys with him so his blind running mate could stay close. He played tennis but had to quit after a fall on the court due to Parkinson's disease.

More than the type of person he was, perhaps his most lasting impact was the type of person he encouraged others to be.

"He pushed you to be the best person you could be," Theg said, "but you never ever doubted that he'd be in your corner."

Farewell to Readers: Lucky Pinky Has the Last Word

Editor's note: Kent Miller, a frequent columnist for the Tallahassee Democrat, died on Aug. 14 at age 89. His family wanted to share this column that he wrote in 2013 as a farewell to his readers.

Most obituaries are deadly, formula-like, the subject squeezed dry by the focus on dates, names, occupation, and style demands of the paper. Most readers would like a more personal portrait, at least some inkling of what made this person tick.

In this context, I challenge you to draft your obituary now, while you are reasonably competent. The process may lead to some insight, and your family will be grateful for not having to write it.

As an example here is my last draft. My critics may complain that this is too personal, too narcissistic. But isn't that the essence of an obituary?

KENT S. MILLER (Nov. 19, 1927 – Aug. 14, 2017).

In high school, he was given the nickname Pinky (his skin color) and later someone amended this to Lucky Pinky (in part because of some minor skill in pool and poker). The nickname Pinky was so widely accepted that at the time of his death the majority of his college classmates could not tell you his first name.

In 1946, as a freshman at William & Mary, he was drafted into the Infantry but his good luck held. Reporting for KP duty at Fort McClellan, Miller mentioned to the Mess Sergeant that he had a generalized skin rash. The Sergeant told him to get the hell out of his kitchen. The medics decided that he was allergic to the wool uniform, and with the war having ended, the world would be safe without him.

For most of his life, Miller was Mr. Everyman, very much in the middle of the pack. In high school, he was second string in football, average half-miler. He regretted not being a better student at William and Mary (academic probation twice) but confessed to having a really good time. Finally, he straightened out enough to earn a PhD. in psychology.

He came to Tallahassee in 1955 and worked as director of a mental health clinic until 1963. Finding satisfaction as a therapist, he recalled the words of one of his last patients, a woman he worked with for months: "I really appreciate all you have done for me, particularly since I didn't have the money to see a real doctor."

At Florida State University he moved through the professorial ranks with relative ease. For the most part, his books were favorably reviewed but modest sellers (he liked to think that the darkness of the subjects may have contributed to this) — e.g., child abuse, death penalty, racial issues, guardianship for the elderly. Comfort was found in Ecclesiastes: of the making of many books there is no end and much study wearies the body....

Miller was not in the middle of the pack when it came to family, embracing Calvin Trillin's observation that any man who does not think his children superior is suspect.

The greatest and most demanding hustle of his life was persuading Betty Davis to marry him. They were unique in being the only couple ever to own three Studebakers.

Towards the end he said that he could die peacefully, knowing that he would not have to see the inside of another cathedral or be served jugged hare.

In his 80s he was asked the question commonly put to old-timers: What have you found to be true and do you have rules to live by?

Nothing you haven't heard before. Have fun. Always have some work to do. Love mightily. You can nearly always find somebody willing to leave a tour to go for a beer. Never get so old that you can't get angry in the face of social injustice. He embraced Gandhi's words: Whatever you do will be insignificant, but it is very important that you do it.

The words he would have liked to be said over his open casket: "Look! He's moving." (Didn't happen. He was cremated.)

Betty and Kent with their eight grandchildren (from left to right) Chris Theg, Elizabeth Riccardi, Shannon Hovick Thigpen, Christina Riccardi, Jessica Hovick, Alex Theg, Sam Theg, & Mary Riccardi Peck, 2011

37388407R00160

Made in the USA
San Bernardino, CA
30 May 2019